# CONTENTS

P9-DGL-892

iii

# LITERATURE MADE EASY

GEORGE ORWELL'S

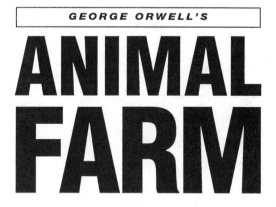

# ANIMAL FARM

Written by LONA McGREGOR
*WITH TONY BUZAN*

**BARRON'S**

First edition for the United States and Canada published by Barron's Educational Series, Inc., 1999.

Copyright © 1999 U.S. version, Barron's Educational Series, Inc.

First published in the United Kingdom by Hodder & Stoughton Ltd. under the title: *A Guide to Animal Farm*

Copyright © 1997 Lona McGregor
Introduction © 1997 Tony Buzan

Cover photograph © The Ronald Grant Archive
Mind Maps: David Orr
Illustrations: Karen Donnelly

Lona McGregor asserts the moral right to be identified as the author of this work.

American text edited by Benjamin Griffith.

*All inquiries should be addressed to:*
Barron's Educational Series, Inc.
250 Wireless Boulevard
Hauppauge, New York 11788
**http://www.barronseduc.com**

ISBN-13: 978-0-7641-0819-8
ISBN-10: 0-7641-0819-0

*Library of Congress Catalog Card No. 98-73081*

PRINTED IN THE UNITED STATES OF AMERICA
9 8 7 6 5

There are five important things you must know about your brain and memory to revolutionize
the way you study:

◆ how your memory
("recall") works *while* you are learning
◆ how your memory works *after* you have finished learning
◆ how to use Mind Maps – a special technique for helping you with all aspects of your studies
◆ how to prepare for tests and exams.

# Recall during learning
## – THE NEED FOR BREAKS

When you are studying, your memory can concentrate, understand, and remember well for between 20 and 45 minutes at a time; then it needs a break. If you carry on for longer than this without a break, your memory starts to break down. If you study for hours nonstop, you will remember only a small fraction of what you have been trying to learn, and you will have wasted hours of valuable time.

So, ideally, *study for less than an hour*, then take a five- to ten-minute break. During the break listen to music, go for a walk, do some exercise, or just daydream. (Daydreaming is a necessary brain-power booster – geniuses do it regularly.) During the break your brain will be sorting out what it has been learning, and you will go back to your books with the new information safely stored and organized in your memory. We recommend breaks at regular intervals as you work through this book. Make sure you take them!

# Recall after learning
## — THE WAVES OF YOUR MEMORY

What do you think begins to happen to your memory right after you have finished learning something? Does it immediately start forgetting? No! Your brain actually *increases* its power and continues remembering. For a short time after your study session, your brain integrates the information, making a more complete picture of everything it has just learned. Only then does the rapid decline in memory begin, and as much as 80 percent of what you have learned can be forgotten in a day.

However, if you catch the top of the wave of your memory, and briefly review (look back over) what you have been studying at the correct time (while your brain is continuing to remember), the memory is imprinted far more strongly, and stays at the crest of the wave for a much longer time. To maximize your brain's power to remember, take a few minutes at the end of a day and use a Mind Map to review what you have learned. Then review it at the end of a week, again at the end of a month, and finally a week before the exams. That way you'll ride your memory wave all the way to your exam – and beyond!

# The Mind Map ®
## — A PICTURE OF THE WAY YOU THINK

Do you like taking notes? More important, do you like having to go back over and learn them before tests or exams? Most students I know certainly do not! And how do you take your notes? Most people take notes on lined paper, using blue or black ink. The result, visually, is boring. And what does your brain do when it is bored? It turns off, tunes out, and goes to sleep! Add a dash of color, rhythm, imagination, and the whole note-taking process becomes much more fun, uses more of your brain's abilities, and improves your recall and understanding.

Generally, your Mind Map is highly personal and need not be understandable to any other person. It mirrors *your* brain. Its purpose is to build up your "memory muscle" by creating images that will help you recall instantly the most important points about the characters and plot sequences in a work of fiction you are studying.

You will find Mind Maps throughout this book. Study them, add some color, personalize them, and then try drawing your own – you'll remember them far better. Stick them in your files and on your walls for a quick-and-easy review of the topic.

### HOW TO DRAW A MIND MAP

1 First of all, briefly examine the Mind Maps and Mini Mind Maps used in this book. What are the common characteristics? All of them use small pictures or symbols, with words branching out from the illustration.

2 Decide which idea or character in the book you want to illustrate and draw a picture, starting in the middle of the page so that you have plenty of room to branch out. Remember that no one expects a young Rembrandt or Picasso here; artistic ability is not as important as creating an image you (and you alone) will remember. A round smiling (or sad) face might work as well in your memory as a finished portrait. Use marking pens of different colors to make your Mind Map as vivid and memorable as possible.

3 As your thoughts flow freely, add descriptive words and other ideas on the colored branching lines that connect to the central image. Print clearly, using one word per line if possible.

4 Further refine your thinking by adding smaller branching lines, containing less important facts and ideas, to the main points.

5 Presto! You have a personal outline of your thoughts about the character and plot. It's not a stodgy formal outline, but a colorful image that will stick in your mind, it is hoped, throughout classroom discussions and final exams.

### HOW TO READ A MIND MAP

1 Begin in the center, the focus of your topic.

2 The words/images attached to the center are like chapter headings; read them next.

3 Always read out from the center, in every direction (even on the left-hand side, where you will have to read from right to left, instead of the usual left to right).

### USING MIND MAPS

Mind Maps are a versatile tool; use them for taking notes in class or from books, for solving problems, for brainstorming with friends, and for reviewing and working for tests or exams – their uses are endless. You will find them invaluable for planning essays for coursework and exams. Number your main branches in the order in which you want to use them and off you go – the main headings for your essay are done and all your ideas are logically organized.

## Helpful hints for studying for exams

◆ Study hard at the start of your course, not the end, and avoid "exam panic." Start to study at the beginning of the course.

◆ Use Mind Maps throughout your course, and build a Master Mind Map for each subject – a giant Mind Map that summarizes everything you know about the subject.

◆ Use memory techniques such as mnemonics (verses or systems for remembering things like dates and events).

◆ Get together with one or two friends to study, compare Mind Maps, and discuss topics.

### AND FINALLY...

Have *fun* while you learn – it has been shown that students who make their studies enjoyable understand and remember everything better and get the highest grades. I wish you and your brain every success! (Tony Buzan)

# HOW TO USE THIS GUIDE

This guide assumes that you have already read *Animal Farm*, although you could read Background and The Story of *Animal Farm* before that. It is best to use the guide alongside the text. You could read the Who's Who? and Themes sections without referring to the novel, but you will get more out of these sections if you do refer to it to check the points made in these sections, and especially when thinking about the questions designed to test your recall and help you think about the novel.

## THE DIFFERENT SECTIONS

The Commentary section can be used in a number of ways. One way is to read a chapter or part of a chapter in the novel, and then read the commentary for that section. Continue until you come to a test yourself section – then take a break. Or, read the Commentary for a chapter or part of a chapter, then read that section in the novel, then go back to the Commentary. Find out what works best for you.

Topics for Discussion and Brainstorming gives topics that could well appear on exams or provide the basis for coursework. It would be particularly useful for you to discuss them with friends, or brainstorm them using Mind Map techniques (see p. vi).

How to Get an "A" in English Literature gives valuable advice on what to look for in a text, and what skills you need to develop in order to achieve your personal best.

The discussion of the exam essay is a useful night-before reminder of how to tackle exam questions, and Model Answer gives an example of an "A"-grade essay and the Mind Map and plan used to write it.

## THE QUESTIONS

Whenever you come across a question in the guide with a star ✪ in front of it, think about it for a moment. You could even jot down a few words to focus your mind. There is not usually a "right" answer to these questions; it is important for you to develop your own opinions if you want to get an "A." The Test Yourself sections are designed to take you about 10–20 minutes each – which will be time well spent.

# Key to icons

### THEMES

A **theme** is an idea explored by an author. Whenever a theme is dealt with in the guide, the appropriate icon is used. This means you can find where a theme is mentioned just by flicking through the book. Go on – try it now!

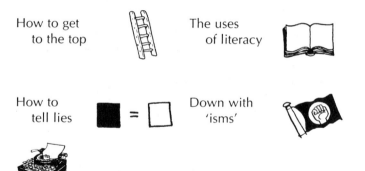

How to get
   to the top

The uses
   of literacy

How to
   tell lies

Down with
   'isms'

### STYLE AND LANGUAGE

This icon is used in the Commentary wherever there is a special section on the author's choice of words and **imagery** (a kind of word picture used to make an idea come alive).

### BROKEN COMMANDMENTS

Additional icons have been used in the Commentary where the Commandments have been broken. For example, where the Sixth Commandment has been broken, the following icon will appear ⟨6⟩

# BACKGROUND

This chapter is about the historical and social context in which Orwell wrote *Animal Farm*. Because the novel is a political **satire** (a work that uses ridicule to expose wickedness or stupidity), it is particularly important for you to have a basic understanding of these things; however, you must always relate your knowledge of the history to the novel itself.

## Animal Farm and the Russian Revolution

*Animal Farm* is based on events during and after the 1917 Russian Revolution, which overthrew the absolute power of the tsar (emperor) and a rigid social system that kept most of the population in great poverty.

The revolutionaries were divided into many different groups, but most of them based their beliefs on the writings of Karl Marx (1818–1883), author of the Communist Manifesto. Almost as soon as the tsar was overthrown, civil war broke out between the revolutionaries themselves. The Bolsheviks – later the Communist party – eventually came out on top. They were led by Lenin (1870–1924) and Trotsky (1879–1940).

When Lenin died there was a power struggle between Trotsky and Joseph Stalin, the General Secretary of the party. Stalin won. Like Snowball, Trotsky was a brilliant intellectual but had little political cunning. He was driven into exile and died in Mexico after being stabbed by one of Stalin's secret agents.

Stalin continued Lenin's campaign to modernize Russian agriculture and industry. He got rid of anyone who stood in his way. By 1929 he had complete control of the party and was backed up by the dreaded KGB, or secret police.

Stalin turned against colleagues who had helped him defeat the Trotskyites.. They were expelled from the party or sentenced and executed after show trials where they confessed to imaginary crimes.

Russia was known as the USSR or Soviet Union until 1991. Even without its empire it is still the largest country in the world, twice the size of the United States.

# When and why Orwell wrote the book

George Orwell (1903–50), novelist and political journalist, wrote *Animal Farm* toward the end of World War II, but he was not able to publish it until the war was over. To the British public, Stalin was "Uncle Joe," the brave leader of a nation that had stood up to the invading armies of Nazi Germany. It was not a good time to criticize Russia and its leader.

Beneath the simple surface of *Animal Farm,* Orwell shows the techniques used by Stalin to pervert the original aims of the 1917 Russian Revolution. Like the pig Napoleon, Stalin rose to power by exiling or killing off his rivals. Eventually, he achieved the same position as the tsar whom the Revolution had tried to replace with a more just system of government.

Why did Orwell feel so strongly about this? The events he criticized had taken place before the war. To understand we must look at his life.

His father was one of the officials who ran India – "the Raj" – when it was still part of the British Empire. Orwell won a scholarship to Eton, the English public school. After leaving it, says Orwell, "I went to Burma and joined the Indian Imperial Police . . . It did not suit me and made me hate Imperialism." Orwell spent several years in Paris and London, taking whatever jobs he could to keep himself fed. Eventually, he was able to earn his living through journalism. He also wrote novels, but they did not sell well until he published *Animal Farm.*

In 1936 Orwell married, just before the civil war broke out in Spain. This war was fought between the left-wing Republican government and right-wing Fascist rebels. Like many European socialists, Orwell and his wife went to Spain to help the government forces.

Most foreigners joined the "International Brigade," but Orwell found himself attached to the Spanish Trotskyists, followers of Leon Trotsky, Stalin's rival in the Communist power struggle that followed the death of Lenin. You can read more about that in *Animal Farm* and the Russian Revolution (p. 1).

In Spain Orwell experienced first-hand the same kind of events as those going on in Russia itself. He wrote:

... when the Communists gained control ... of the Spanish Government and began to hunt down the Trotskyists, we both found ourselves among the victims. We were very lucky to get out of Spain alive. ...

These manhunts in Spain went on at the same time as the great purges in the USSR. . .

*Animal Farm* was written to make people wake up to the truth about Stalin. It seems strange today that the facts took so long to emerge, but we must remember that these events took place before television and modern telecommunications were available to many people.

At first, Orwell could not think of a form simple enough to be understood by everyone, then, while he was living in a small village, he saw a huge cart horse being whipped along a narrow path by a 10-year-old boy:

It struck me that if only such animals became aware of their strength we should have no power over them, and that men exploit animals in much the same way as the rich exploit the proletariat.

Those two thoughts expanded into the main theme of *Animal Farm* and the tragic story of Boxer.

The book would not have been such a huge success if it had been about only one ruthless political leader. Through Napoleon/Stalin Orwell examines the methods that unscrupulous leaders use to acquire power over people and how they abuse it. He was writing about the world of politics. What he has to say applies to every social group or institution where some people wish to be *more equal than others.*

# Why animals?

Stories about animals have been popular in every period of human history. Those that show them talking and behaving like human beings are known as **fables**. Their modern version exists in Disney films and cartoons.

A fable is not really about animals, but about us. It takes certain animal qualities and expresses them in human terms. It tries to teach a lesson about human nature and the conditions of human life. The audience is amused by the story and more likely to pay attention to its real point – the "moral."

3

When Orwell adapted *Animal Farm* as a radio play, he wrote, "I meant the moral to be that revolutions only effect a radical improvement when the masses are alert and know how to chuck out their leaders as soon as the latter have done their job."

❂ At what point do you think the animals ought to have "chucked out" their pig leaders? Later you will read what Orwell himself wrote about this question.

Fables, fairy tales, and folk tales share certain features. There is always a clear story line. The question, "What happened next"? keeps us listening or reading to the end. Repeated actions – slightly different each time – help to pull the story together.

Fables have no long descriptions that might distract us from the main plot. The characters are less complicated than those in a novel or play. They are "types," rather than real individuals. They live in a simple world, but it is full of down-to-earth, everyday detail. The characters are divided into "good" and "bad" in a way that is not true in real life.

You will find all these features in *Animal Farm*, although the story carries a much more complicated message than any fable or fairy tale. Orwell's farm is one of the small, general type much more common in his own time than in ours. Every species of farm animal is found there, though not in large numbers.

The farm represents Russian society after the Revolution. Its animals personify different social groups and the way they used or abused their opportunities to make a new start. By writing about animals rather than human beings, Orwell was also able to illustrate the rise of certain groups in Soviet society.

### Assignments and questions

? Make a Mind Map of the historical background to *Animal Farm*.

? How do animal cartoons differ from real-life documentaries about animal behavior? Why do you think they are so popular?

? Make a list of the characteristics of animal fables. Give one example of each from *Animal Farm*.

# THE STORY OF *ANIMAL FARM*

## Unrest

Mr. Jones, the owner of Manor Farm, has become lazy and taken to drink. One night, his animals meet secretly in the barn to hear Old Major, the prize boar, describe his dream of a world fit for animals.

He tells them they could exchange their miserable way of life for happiness and freedom if only they could get rid of Man. Man steals what the animals produce and lives in luxury off their labor. Major wants them to work for the great Rebellion. All animals must be comrades in the fight against their enemy, Man.

Major gives a list of human habits that the animals should avoid. He ends by singing "Beasts of England," an old song that looks forward to *the golden future time.*

Major dies three days later, and the animals prepare themselves for the uprising. They are led by the pigs, who turn Major's ideas into a complete way of thinking they call *Animalism.* Some of the other animals have great difficulty in understanding its ideas.

# The Seven Commandments

**THESE ARE THE SEVEN COMMANDMENTS OF ANIMALISM. REFER TO THE NOVEL TO SEE HOW THEY ARE BROKEN AND ALTERED AS THE BOOK PROGRESSES.**

**1** WHATEVER GOES UPON TWO LEGS IS AN ENEMY

Napoleon begins to trade with humans
Squealer walks on hind legs
Humans visit Animal Farm

**2** WHATEVER GOES UPON FOUR LEGS, OR HAS WINGS, IS A FRIEND

Dogs attack Snowball
Dogs attack Boxer

**3** NO ANIMAL SHALL WEAR CLOTHES

Napoleon puts on Mr. Jones' hat
Pigs wear human clothes

**4**  NO ANIMAL SHALL SLEEP IN A BED

pigs sleep in farmhouse
    beds

**5**  NO ANIMAL SHALL DRINK ALCOHOL

Pigs begin to drink beer and
    whiskey

**6**  NO ANIMAL SHALL KILL ANY OTHER
ANIMAL

Hens starved to death
Pigs, hens, and sheep executed
Boxer sent to the slaughterhouse

**7**  ALL ANIMALS ARE EQUAL

Pigs take milk and apples
Pigs get up one hour later than
    others
rations reduced except for pigs and
    dogs

## The Rebellion

The Rebellion breaks out very suddenly. One day, goaded by hunger, the animals fight back when Mr. Jones and his men try to keep them from the food bins. After driving away the humans, they set themselves up as the democratic community called Animal Farm.

The principles of Animalism are set out in Seven Commandments painted on the far wall of the barn.

The first harvest is a great success. When Jones attempts to recover his farm, the animals defeat him at the Battle of the Cowshed.

## The rise of the pigs

Things start to go wrong when the quick-witted pigs find they can take advantage of their comrades. They begin with minor acts of greed and end up with open exploitation and murder. The main purpose of the story is to show how the pigs become corrupted by their power.

## Snowball versus Napoleon

Quite soon the unity of the pigs is disrupting in a struggle between two boars, Snowball and Napoleon. Snowball is full of schemes to improve the farm. He, at least, intends to share the benefits with everyone. His rival, Napoleon, is interested only in acquiring supreme power. He drives Snowball away by force and then imposes a reign of terror on Animal Farm. He is backed up by his propaganda agent, Squealer, who uses lies and mind-bending techniques to keep the animals ignorant about what is being done to them.

## Full circle

One by one the Seven Commandments are broken by the pigs and then reworded to conform to the wishes of Napoleon. By the end of the book the situation has come full circle. Animal

Farm has gone back to its old name of Manor Farm, the pigs are trading with the neighboring farmers, and the other animals are as exploited as ever.

One evening, the animals crowd around the farmhouse windows to watch the pigs and their human guests feasting together. As they gaze from pig to man and man to pig the features of both seem to merge, and it becomes impossible to say which is which.

---

To fix the story in your mind, try this **mnemonic** (memory aid):

**R**ebellion **E**nds **A**s **D**isaster.

**A**rrogant **N**apoleon **I**nflicts **M**isery.

**A**nimal **L**aborers **F**eebly **A**cquiesce.

**R**eturn of **M**anor Farm!

### READ ANIMAL FARM

---

# **W**HO'S WHO?

# **T**he main animal characters

Orwell gives each of his animals the nature traditionally associated with it in fables and folklore: The donkey is stubborn, sheep are stupid, pigs are greedy, and so on. Here each creature also stands for a side of human nature that the story tries to demonstrate. Although Orwell's main characters are more developed than this, they do not reveal as much of themselves as is usual in a novel.

Taken as a whole, however, his simple animal figures are far more complicated than those in fables. Animal Farm stands for the whole of human society, particularly Russian society after the Revolution. The way in which the animals interact with each other is more important to Orwell's story than their nature as individuals.

## Old Major

Old Major appears only in Chapter 1 but *his soul goes marching on.* He is a majestic old boar respected by all, and his speech to the animals leads directly to the great Rebellion. He makes them aware of the injustices they suffer and fills them with the hope of a better life.

Major is wise and benevolent and wants only to help his fellow animals. ✪ Is there anything in the **character** of his speech that points forward to the methods used by Squealer? His thoughts are carefully presented to play on the animals' feelings. Notice that he calls the animals together to listen to the description of a *dream*. ✪ Is Orwell making some comment here about all grand schemes intended to alter human society?

Major represents both Marx and Lenin, the two great thinkers who developed the doctrines of Communism. In fact his speech is a detailed and witty parody of the main ideas of the Communist system. Major's skull is displayed and venerated after his death just as Lenin's embalmed body was put on view in Red Square, Moscow.

## Test yourself

Make sure you know the main points in Major's speech and the way they are connected to the Seven Commandments.

## Napoleon

While Old Major represents the two founders of Communism, Napoleon stands for Joseph Stalin, the Russian dictator who rose to power after Lenin's death. His name is meant to remind us that all totalitarian leaders use more or less the same methods to reach their position of strength and stay there.

We first meet Napoleon in Chapter 2 as a *large, rather fierce looking Berkshire boar with a reputation for getting his own way*. His silence and strength of will contrast with Snowball's liveliness and endless flow of ideas. Like most dictators he rises to power in two stages: First he becomes one of a privileged class – the pigs – and then he seizes power from his rivals.

To begin with, the differences between Snowball and Napoleon seem quite helpful. They make a good team and work together to put the ideas of Animalism into practice.

Napoleon's practical good sense leads him to deal with what started off the Rebellion in the first place – the animals' raging hunger. His first action is to give them double rations from the storage shed.

Napoleon stands shoulder to shoulder with Snowball when they push their way into the empty farmhouse. He sends for the paint that Snowball uses to change the name on the five-barred gate. His true character begins to show when he stays behind to drink the milk while the others go out to the fields to begin the hay harvest; however, a first-time reader might well put this down to sheer greed. We expect pigs to be greedy.

The first signs of rivalry between the two boars shows up at the Sunday meetings. Neither will agree to the other's proposals. Napoleon takes away the puppies, saying that it is more important to educate the young than those already grown up. Is this done out of jealousy of Snowball or does he have some more sinister motive? At the time it could be either. The truth does not come out until much later.

Napoleon seems to take no part in the Battle of the Cowshed. It is won through the courage and clever strategy of Snowball. By winter the two pigs are quarreling violently over every item that comes up at the meetings. The climax is reached when Snowball's plans for the windmill are on the point of being put to the vote. Napoleon calls in his dogs to drive Snowball off the farm.

From now on, Napoleon's behavior becomes more and more ruthless. The animals have already been divided into two classes – pigs with some extra privileges, and the others. Now, with the help of his supporters, Napoleon deliberately sets out to exploit the animals for his own benefit. He controls them through terror – the executions, threats of Jones' return, lies, and brainwashing. There is more about this in the sections, "How to Get to the Top" and "How to Tell Lies."

Napoleon's character gets worse as time goes on. The Commandments are changed and finally abolished to suit him. His behavior changes to fit the new image of someone lifted up to an almost godlike level. He stays indoors, confident that his orders will be carried out by his followers. Inside the farmhouse he has special privileges. There is a lot of ceremony when he does appear in public. He awards himself medals, and the animals are encouraged to give him flattering titles when they mention him. His children are given a share in his exclusive privileges.

Napoleon is outsmarted by Frederick over the sale of the wood. He has been going back and forth between the two humans in a desperate search for the better price. This clownish behavior ought to make the animals less afraid of him but they are too subdued to question him by now, so in fact, it only confuses them more. This, in turn, makes them even more vulnerable to manipulation. Napoleon's brutality is summed up in his treatment of Boxer. He feels no pity or gratitude toward this faithful, hard-working horse when he falls ill. Boxer is sold to a horse slaughter, and the profit on his carcass is spent on more whiskey for the pigs.

Napoleon's total corruption is most strikingly shown by the way the pigs and human beings merge into the same creature. After breaking all the rules of Animalism, Napoleon begins to walk on two legs, carry a whip, wear clothes, and adopt a human lifestyle. His attitude toward the animals is even worse than that of Farmer Jones.

**Over to you**

Make a set of icons for the different methods used by Napoleon to acquire power and keep it, for example taking control of the rations and removing the puppies. Make a Mind Map for yourself.

## Snowball

Snowball represents Trotsky, Stalin's great rival, who was forced into exile and eventually assassinated by Stalin's agents.

Snowball completely overshadows Napoleon until the end of Chapter 5. He is energetic, fast-talking, and bubbling with ideas. With Napoleon and Squealer he develops Major's ideas into the system of Animalism. We can be fairly certain that Snowball would take the lead in the pigs' discussions.

Snowball has a very clear idea of what is needed to make the Rebellion work: The animals must be educated into understanding the new system; they must form committees and learn to read and write.

Up to a point Snowball can adapt himself to those who are not as intelligent as himself. He is patient with Mollie's silly questions, and he sees the importance of *reducing the principles of Animalism to seven commandments.* For the benefit of the hens, ducks, and sheep he produces the slogan *Four legs good, two legs bad.*

Snowball is not just a thinker, an "intellectual"; he is a good organizer as well. Like Trotsky he has a great military mind. His clever planning is responsible for the animals' victory in the Battle of the Cowshed.

The way that Snowball works for the good of all is in sharp contrast with Napoleon's selfish concern for nobody but himself; however, we must not see Snowball as entirely virtuous. He unites with the other pigs to keep the milk and apples.

Snowball also has weaknesses as a leader. He cannot see the damage being caused by his disputes with Napoleon. His schemes for improving the farm go far beyond its practical needs. They are also far beyond the animals' grasp.

Snowball becomes completely obsessed with the windmill project and spends hours alone with his drawings. His design for the windmill turns into an end in itself, rather than something to be judged on its usefulness to the farm.

It is not surprising then that Snowball is completely unaware of Napoleon's plans to get rid of him. He makes no attempt to fight back but runs for his life.

Although Snowball disappears from the story in Chapter 5, he still has an influence on events at Animal Farm. The questions below will help fix him in your mind.

## Test yourself

?   Before your final review look at the PIG PEDESTAL (p. 45) and decide whether you need to put other incidents into the diagram.

? Compare Snowball and Napoleon by making separate Mind Maps of what you know about their characters (not their actions). How would each of these qualities help them rise to the top? As far as you can, give your information in pictures not words.

? Looking at your Mind Maps can you say what was the most important cause of Napoleon's triumph over Snowball?

## Squealer

Think of the most persuasive person you know. ❸ What techniques of persuasion does this person use? Keep these in mind as you read about Squealer.

*The others said of Squealer that he could turn black into white.* This joke turns into a terrible truth as the story unfolds. Squealer is a fat little pig who represents the less obvious methods used by corrupt governments to keep their people under control.

Through him Orwell shows that dictators stay in power by sharing some of their privileges with a small group, the "elite." In return, these followers will control or wipe out other people for the dictator. They act out of self-interest and fear of losing what they have. They accept the dictator's own greater privileges for the same reasons.

The pigs represent this elite group. We see them through the eyes of the animals, and we know that Napoleon, Snowball and Squealer are the most important. We do not know how the others relate to each other or who gives commands to whom. This makes them more frightening because they all appear to have the same collective power.

Squealer himself becomes more important after Snowball has been driven from the farm. His duty is to explain – or rather explain *away* – the changes made by Napoleon to the running of the farm. Whenever he appears, we can be sure that some twisting of the facts will follow.

Sometimes Squealer tells straightforward lies, such as "The windmill was really Napoleon's idea" or "Snowball has sold himself to Frederick." Squealer also hides the truth by his use of words. When the animals are given smaller food rations, this is not called a reduction, but a *readjustment*. In the same spirit, he uses statistics to persuade the animals that life is getting better and better. The animals believe him, even against the evidence of their own hunger and exhaustion.

Half-truths are another of Squealer's powerful weapons. Snowball *did* flee at the Battle of the Cowshed, but it was a tactic to lure the enemy into the yard. To trade with humans is obviously against the whole idea of Animalism, but Squealer justifies it by pointing out that there is no Commandment forbidding animals to trade.Squealer is, of course, involved in rewriting the Seven Commandments. He justifies this with glib arguments and personally adds the extra words that change their meaning.

He also uses a technique known as brainwashing or psychological warfare. He turns the animals' own fears against them. If they do not agree with the new arrangements, Jones will come back. Knowing that most of the animals have poor memories he forces them to accept his own version of past events. The most striking example is the way he alters their opinion of Snowball.

Our dislike of Squealer mounts as the story goes on. His callousness and abuse of power increase at the same rate as Napoleon's. The worst instance occurs when Boxer is sent to the slaughterhouse. Squealer invents his most detailed fiction ever to dupe the animals and seems to enjoy doing it. After Snowball's disappearance, Squealer becomes the most important figure in Napoleon's inner circle.

### A quick exercise

? Make a Mind Map of Squealer's appearances and note what happens each time. Try to do this with picture symbols and make your word notes as brief as possible. You will find this another good way to fix the "shape" of the story in your mind.

? Make use of the section on How to Tell Lies at the same time. Think up a simple sign to represent each of the techniques discussed. How many examples of each can you remember?

## Boxer

Boxer is the opposite of everything represented by Napoleon and the pigs. He is loyal, honest, and kind. Even when fighting he is sorry for the stable boy he hurts. He stands for ordinary workers – the proletariat. Revolutions are made in their name but they often benefit very little from the change.

Animal Farm survives because of Boxer's enormous strength and hard work. It would have been impossible to build the windmill without him. In the days of Jones he is *universally respected for his steadiness of character and tremendous powers of work*. Under the rule of the pigs he is far more exploited than he ever was by Farmer Jones, yet, in his own way Boxer represents as dangerous an extreme as Napoleon. He meets all difficult situations with his two slogans – *"I will work harder!"* and *"Napoleon is always right'."* These are a substitute for actual thinking. The first causes Boxer literally to work himself to death. The pigs make no effort to stop him and he ignores the warnings of Clover and Benjamin.

None of the animals except Benjamin sees what Napoleon is doing to them. Boxer's own failure to understand has serious consequences both for himself and for the other animals, who look up to him.

When Boxer has the dog at his mercy, he waits for instructions from Napoleon. He is unaware that it was Napoleon who ordered the dogs to attack him because he took so long to admit that Snowball was a traitor.

After the executions Boxer does not stay with the other animals on the knoll. They at least face up to their terror and misery and try to console each other. Boxer trots away to haul more stones from the quarry.

17

Even when he has collapsed from overwork, he still believes in the myth of his retirement. Perhaps "they" will let Benjamin retire too to be his companion. In fact, none of the animals will ever retire.

We are outraged at the way Boxer is exploited, but we may also be irritated that he cannot see through Napoleon. We want him to resent the unfairness of life at Animal Farm. The scene where he is taken away to the slaughterer is the grimmest in the book. We hate Napoleon on Boxer's behalf because Boxer himself is unable to hate him.

Orwell is doing this to us quite deliberately. Through the character of Boxer he is trying to make us face up to the unpleasant truth that ruthless leaders can always exploit the goodwill of others.

## Benjamin

Benjamin is the most perceptive animal on the farm – also the oldest. He will probably outlive them all – *None of you has ever seen a dead donkey.* Bad-tempered and pessimistic, he never shirks his work but does no more than he has to. The others can never persuade him to say what he thinks about the Rebellion. We get the impression that Benjamin expects it to turn out badly from the start.

By joining the reading and writing classes Benjamin becomes as literate as the pigs. He is not taken in by Squealer's propaganda. When Frederick launches his attack, Benjamin is the only one to realize what is going to happen to the windmill. He seems almost pleased when Frederick blows it up with gunpowder.

Benjamin is the intelligent outsider, the person who "does not want to get involved." ❂ Why doesn't he share his knowledge with the other animals? Is it because he believes it would make no difference in the end? ❂ Do you think it is the moral duty of someone in his position to speak out?

Benjamin is deeply devoted to Boxer. When the slaughterer's van arrives to take the horse away Benjamin loses control. He cannot hold back his rage at the stupidity of the animals as they crowd around to shout out their good-byes.

After Boxer's death Benjamin is *more morose and taciturn than ever.*

## Clover

Clover understands the events at Animal Farm more clearly than Boxer does. Although she realizes the horror of what is going on, she is not clever enough to see where the blame lies.

Clover's warm, motherly nature draws the animals to her. At the first meeting she protects the ducklings *with her great foreleg* against the weight and size of the other animals. After the massacre in the farmyard, they huddle around Clover for comfort.

She feels deep grief that the animals' dreams and hopes have turned out so badly. All the same she will go on working hard and obeying orders. Squealer's propaganda has been 100 percent successful with Clover. *She knew that even as things were they were far better off ... that before all else it was needful to prevent the return of the human beings.*

Between them Boxer and Clover represent the everyday decency and virtues of ordinary people who are betrayed by the revolutionary leaders.

# The other animals

The other animals are not as important to the story as the main characters. All the same, when you are thinking about *Animal Farm* as a political fable, you should look at them carefully. Orwell uses them to show that revolutions can fail for several reasons, not just because leaders are greedy and corrupt.
✪ What attitudes do you think they represent?

## Mollie

Mollie is Mr. Jones' pretty white mare. She represents the rich and idle Russian aristocracy. She is vain and selfish, interested only in ribbons and lumps of sugar. Any system of government suits her so long as it lets her keep her "perks." Unlike the pigs, she does not actively seek advantages over the other animals. She becomes dishonest while trying to hang onto her little luxuries. The Rebellion is not for her! She runs away, just like those Russian aristocrats who fled into exile when revolution broke out.

19

## Muriel

Muriel the goat is quick-witted and soon learns to read. She is upset when told that "Beasts of England" is to be abolished, but that is as far as her protest goes. She pokes around the rubbish heap for scraps of newspaper, which she reads to the other animals without picking out what is important and what is not. Laziness makes her waste her intellect on silly trifles. Orwell is obviously hitting out at people who could understand what is happening around them if they tried, but are not prepared to make the effort.

## The sheep

The sheep are not separate individuals; They act in one mass. They like the sound of their own voices and bleat out the slogan given to them by Snowball for hours on end. They are just as happy with Squealer's opposite version.

## The dogs

The dogs can be classified as minor characters, but they are as important as Napoleon himself to the main theme of *Animal Farm*. The most obvious sign of Napoleon's power and brutality is his bodyguard of nine brass-collared dogs. No names are given to them. They are monsters created by Napoleon from Jessie and Bluebell's puppies. In terms of the fable they stand for Stalin's notorious Secret Police.

## Moses

The raven Moses is *Mr Jones' especial pet ... a spy and a tale-bearer* (p. 10). He has a perch in the farmhouse kitchen and distracts the animals from working for the Rebellion with his talk of Sugarcandy Mountain. When the Rebellion breaks out, Moses follows the Jones family in their flight and then returns unexpectedly just before the death of Boxer.

Moses represents the Russian Orthodox Church. Religion was banned under the Communist regime, but Stalin changed this policy for a short time for political reasons. Moses is named after the great Biblical figure who brought the Ten Commandments down from Mount Sinai, but Moses the raven behaves very differently from his namesake, the great Jewish leader. This raven's tale about Sugarcandy Mountain is Orwell's tool in criticizing the influence of organized religion on society.

## The humans

There are five humans: Mr. and Mrs. Jones of Manor Farm, Pilkington of Foxwood, Frederick of Pinchfield, and the solicitor Whymper. They are not very different from each other, and they have no dialogue. Their conversations are reported only. They are convenient figures to personify the enemy, Man.

The Joneses stand for the *Capitalists*, the owners of property and wealth. According to Communist doctrine, the Capitalists stole the produce of their labor from the *Proletariat,* the ordinary working people. The Joneses also represent the Romanovs, the imperial family deposed and murdered during the Russian Revolution.

Frederick and Pilkington – who represent Germany and Britain – are symbols for the behavior of other nations toward Communist Russia in the early years after the Revolution.

*take a break before moving on to the next section. To help you get to know the main characters of the book, there is a Mind Map on the next page*

21

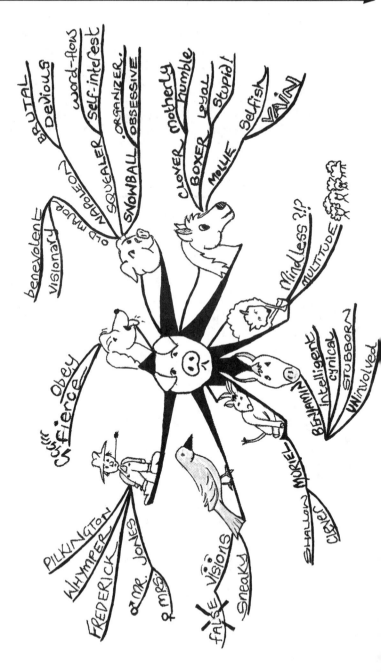

BRUTAL
Devious
word-flows
Self-interest
ORGANIZER
OBSESSIVE
SNOWBALL
SQUEALER
NAPOLEON
Clover motherly
Humble
Boxer loyal
Stupid!
Mollie Selfish
VAIN
old Major
benevolent
visionary

Mindless ?!?
MULTITUDE

BENJAMIN
Intelligent
cynical
STUBBORN
UNinvolved

Obey
Fierce

SHEEP MURIEL
CLEVER
Shallow

PILKINGTON
WHYMPER
FREDERICK
♂ MR. JONES
♀ MRS.

FALSE Visions
Sneaky

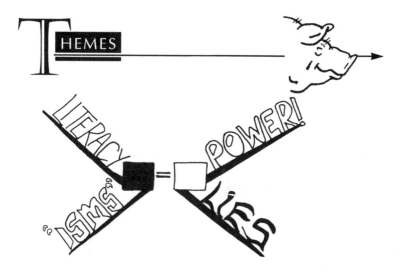

THEMES

## How to get to the top

This section and the two that follow answer an important
question: How do leaders like Napoleon acquire such
enormous power? How individuals and groups get power, keep
it, and become corrupted by it is a major theme in this novel.

## *O*rganization

The first part of the answer is that they rarely do it in one step.
Napoleon already belongs to a group with advantages over the
other animals. The pigs are clever, and they have taught
themselves to read and write. In human terms Napoleon has
attached himself to an organization that plans to get things
changed or influence people in some way.

At first he fits in with what the other pigs are doing. He helps
Squealer and Snowball to work out the principles of Animalism
and teach it to the other animals. Later, he helps them paint the
Seven Commandments on the barn wall.

However, right from the start Napoleon is looking for chances
to get his own way. His first act after the Rebellion is to take

charge of the food supplies. He drinks the milk while everyone else – including the pigs – is busy with the harvest.

# Elitism

Soon, other pigs besides Napoleon are stealing food from the animals. The farm's total yield of milk and apples goes to the pigs. In the end so does the barley. Being greedy himself, Napoleon knows he can use their greed to build up a group of followers who will carry out his orders. This is essential to the rise of a dictator. Protesters will be thrown out of the group. See what happens to the four young porkers.

# Violence

Snowball's plans become so complicated that Napoleon can no longer hope to control them. He stops pretending to cooperate with Snowball, and increasingly bitter disputes break out between the two pigs. This is a power struggle that only one can win. Napoleon falls back on violence and unleashes his vicious dogs. He has been preparing for this day since he took the dogs from their mothers. His real intentions become clear. when he orders them to chase Snowball off the farm.

# Power and privilege

Once in power, Napoleon has no need to make a show of consulting the animals; he can do what he likes. He divides his time between acquiring even more privileges and reinforcing his position. The first is due to Napoleon's greed and vanity. He appears less and less often in public and when he does is surrounded by attendants. He awards himself medals, he has more beer than the other pigs, and eats food that even they are not allowed.

# Overcoming resistance

The second arises from the need to make himself too impressive for anyone to defy him or try to take his place. Napoleon's dogs are the soldiers or secret police that keep an eye on those who might conspire against the dictator.

People can be controlled by fear of consequences. Napoleon starves the hens into returning to their nesting boxes. By the time nine have died, the others are ready to give in. Soon after that he carries out the terrible executions in the farmyard.

✪ Why does no one try to stop Napoleon before it is too late? Note the way the animals react to his rise to power. Most of them are too trusting and too unassertive. They do not question the right of the pigs to take charge. Again, in human terms, they are not intelligent or educated enough to realize what is happening to them. They have no tradition of making decisions for themselves. See The Uses of Literacy for one possible explanation.

There are moments when some of the animals *would have protested* but their voices and even their thoughts are blotted out by the sheep bleating, *"Four legs good, two legs bad!"*. The sheep chant their slogan mindlessly and can be made to do whatever pleases Napoleon. They can outshout any protest through their sheer numbers. At the end of the story their slogan has changed to its opposite, *"Four legs good, two legs better!"*.

Hitler's Nazi party began as a small nationalist group that finally ruled all of Germany. One of its strongest weapons was the use of chanting at huge crowd rallies. A dictator does not get into power through relying on his followers and his secret police alone. The people must be trained to believe what he tells them. That is where Squealer comes in.

## How to tell lies    ■ = ☐

Another major theme in *Animal Farm* is persuasion. The information given out by a group to persuade people to support its point of view is called **propaganda**. The information can be true, partly true, or completely untrue.

Squealer is Napoleon's propaganda agent. He spreads lies by talking to the animals personally, but he stands for all the media that issue propaganda: printed paper, political speeches, film, television, and radio. The simplest form of propaganda is to lie with confidence. This works because most of the time we believe what others tell us. Squealer uses several well-known propaganda techniques, outlined under the following headings:

# Long words and "scientific" explanations

The pigs need milk and apples for their health. They say, *"Tactics, comrades, tactics!,"* when Napoleon decides to build the windmill after all.

# Arguing at the animals' level

He also does the opposite. Most of the animals cannot understand **theories** and **concepts**. They cannot see the link between particular details and the principles of Animalism. They hang on to simple phrases, such as Boxer's *"I will work harder!"* Squealer exploits their inability to generalize to prove to the animals that they are wrong.

When they feel *a vague uneasiness* that Napoleon has decided to start trading, Squealer points out that there is no *written* Commandment forbidding the use of trade and money. He leaves out the fact that Major told them to have nothing to do with Man.

Here is another example. The animals have already agreed that pigs are allowed to live in the farmhouse. Now they are worried over what is really only a minor detail – that the pigs are sleeping in *beds*. These were forbidden in the Fourth Commandment, but *with sheets* has been added to it. Squealer gives another meaning to the word *beds* and protests that the pigs do not use sheets.

# Changing the way people judge events

Boxer says winning the Battle of the Windmill only allows the animals to keep what they already had. Squealer insists that it is a great victory. The celebrations are so splendid that the animals are convinced he is right.

# Brainwashing

Propaganda slides easily into something much more serious – brainwashing. This means altering the whole content of what people think. The most striking example in *Animal Farm* is what happens to the animals' memory of Snowball. They are told that he is a traitor, responsible for the collapse of the windmill, and siding with their enemies. They begin to believe these lies.

Squealer then wipes out their memory of Snowball's bravery at the Battle of the Cowshed. He makes them remember his own version.

# Confusion and terror

Squealer has always backed up his lies with threats that Jones may return. The confusion he has set up in the animals' minds is a weapon in itself. It makes them even more afraid and unsure of what they remember. They begin to see Snowball as *some kind of invisible influence, pervading the air about them and menacing them with all kinds of dangers.*

When people reach this stage they make up rumors for themselves. They do the dictator's work for him. ○ Which of the rumors come from Squealer and which from the animals themselves?

# Learning to hate the enemy

Giving people someone to hate is a good way to unite them. This is the reason for wartime propaganda and it also was behind Hitler's campaign against the Jewish people in the 1930s and 1940s. In *Animal Farm* Old Major wants the animals to hate Man so they will have the courage to rise against him, but Napoleon wants to unite the animals against Snowball so that he can control them more easily.

In human society people are often intolerant toward those who are different from them in color, religion, language, race, or lifestyle. (This has often been portrayed in literature, as in Shakespeare's play *The Merchant of Venice*.) ○ How might a politician make use of this intolerance?

### Test yourself

You have read about the way that power can be acquired and how people are persuaded to accept leaders who behave like tyrants. Now try to answer the questions on the next page.

**?**    Can you think of examples of groups formed for some definite purpose? They could range from fund-raising charities to paramilitary terrorist groups.

**?**    What groups in human society would you say are the equivalents of the pigs, the dogs, and the sheep in *Animal Farm*?

## The uses of literacy

To be "literate" means to be "acquainted with letters," for example, able to read and write. *By the autumn almost every animal on the farm was literate in some degree.* They have learned to recognize certain words and letters, but they cannot read easily and most of them cannot write at all. To be fully literate someone must be able to do both.

For the majority there was little point in being able to read before the invention of printing. ✪ Can you say why? Even after the appearance of printed text, rulers felt no obligation to educate their people, In fact, there were strong political pressures against it. This did not change until the nineteenth century, with compulsory state education. ✪ Again, can you use your knowledge of history to suggest reasons?

Orwell's interest in literacy arose from his strongly held belief that people had the right to know what their leaders were up to. He thought that the best way to achieve this was by giving them access to information, and in his day this meant mainly printed information.

In *Animal Farm* he looks at the question of literacy in several ways. Snowball genuinely does want the animals to be able to read; it is he who sets up the reading and writing classes and paints the Seven Commandments on the end wall of the barn. If more animals had been fully literate they would have realized sooner that the wording of the Commandments had changed. ✪ Do you think this would have made them less passive about letting the pigs take over? ✪ Why were so many of the animals unable to become literate? (Don't simply say, "Animals can't learn to read and write!" For the purposes of this fable we have to assume they can.)

However, there is more to literacy than merely being able to read and write, as Orwell points out what the animals do with this skill, if they acquire it. Each of them stands for a type of reader – those skimming over anything that meets the eye (Muriel), those reading only what reinforces their own beliefs (the dogs), those reading only what is easy and amusing (Mollie). They are literate, but not *functionally* literate; they learn to read, but do not read to learn. (Benjamin is in a class of his own. His refusal to use his ability is part of his whole dislike of becoming involved.)

People who read in an indiscriminate and uncritical way run the risk of having their skill turned against them. By the time Orwell wrote *Animal Farm*, literacy had become so general in Europe that it could be used to suppress the truth rather than spread it around. During World War II both sides used "disinformation" to encourage their own side and dishearten the enemy. Newspapers were strictly censored and airplanes flying over hostile territory dropped millions of leaflets as well as bombs.

In the same way, the growing power of the pigs is backed up by changes in the wording of the Seven Commandments, which Muriel reads to the other animals. Because she has never thought about what she reads, she believes that these are the original commandments, and so do the others. What is written must be true, right?

## Down with "isms"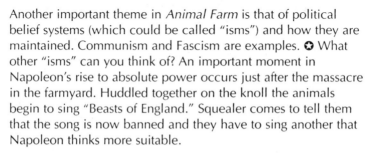

Another important theme in *Animal Farm* is that of political belief systems (which could be called "isms") and how they are maintained. Communism and Fascism are examples. ✪ What other "isms" can you think of? An important moment in Napoleon's rise to absolute power occurs just after the massacre in the farmyard. Huddled together on the knoll the animals begin to sing "Beasts of England." Squealer comes to tell them that the song is now banned and they have to sing another that Napoleon thinks more suitable.

If you look at the words of "Beasts of England" you may wonder what Napoleon objects to, apart from the fact that the song does not glorify him. Probably he does not want them to be reminded of the early days after the Rebellion at which time they were free and equal – almost.

Flags, music, and songs have a very strong effect on people. They remind them of the way they felt the last time they saw and heard them, and call up the same emotions. Public displays of this kind can also be used to reinforce the power of one group in the community or to stir up hatred against those the group considers its enemies. The situation that exists when a group or individual manages to suppress all discussion of opposite views is known as **totalitarianism**.

At Animal Farm the green flag is run up every Sunday morning after breakfast. This helps to strengthen the animals' pride in what they have done and their sense of belonging together.

After the Battle of the Cowshed they award themselves medals and set up a gun at the flagpole to fire on special occasions. When Napoleon takes over, the scale and purpose of these ceremonies change into a dictator's weapon, but the animals do not realize that they are now ruled by a totalitarian dictator. *What with the songs, the processions, ... the thunder of the gun ... they were able to forget that their bellies were empty, at least part of the time.*

The "isms" that Orwell saw come to power in the 1930s – Fascism in Spain and Italy, Stalinism in Russia, Nazism in Germany – all made great use of processions and music. These movements grew in strength and numbers because (a) their propaganda convinced so many people, and (b) the rest ignored the danger until it was too late to resist.

The film *Cabaret*, set in 1930s Germany, sums up this process in a single scene. In a crowded beer garden a boy who has joined the Hitler Youth stands up to sing a Nazi song. His fresh young face and the lilt of the song are very appealing. A few people rise to their feet and join in with enthusiasm. Gradually, more and more of them stand up until those left sitting feel they have to do the same. Finally, everyone in the beer garden is singing the song, whether they want to or not.

*study the Mind Map (opposite), which summarizes the themes in Animal Farm, then take a break before thinking about Orwell's style*

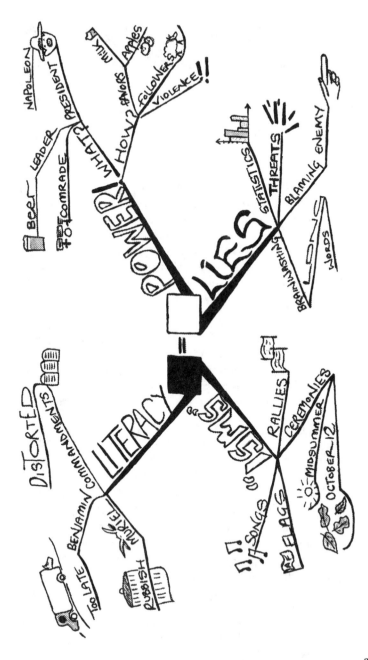

31

# LANGUAGE, STYLE, AND STRUCTURE

## *J*ust words?

The Test Yourself sections in the Commentary suggest passages you should look at in detail. This section refers to some general points about Orwell's style.

Orwell felt very strongly that writers should express themselves in strong, direct language. "Good prose is like a window-pane," he said in his *Collected Essays*. Writers should not use long words where short words would do, or more words than necessary, and they should cut out adverbs like *beautifully* or *horribly* – unless they added something to the meaning of a sentence. He detested wornout images, such as "white as snow," and any showy, unnecessarily ornate or fancy use of words.

You will find that Orwell keeps to his own rules. *Animal Farm* does contain some old agricultural words you may not have come across before but that were well known in Orwell's own lifetime, but otherwise the story is told so plainly that any imagery or descriptive detail is all the more effective.

Notice particularly the following: the entry of Boxer and Clover with *their vast hairy hooves*, the inside of the farmhouse, Boxer dragging stones to the top of the quarry, the executions, the two occasions when the animals gather on the knoll.

There are also passages where Orwell deliberately breaks into what is called **jargon** – technical language that only those familiar with a subject will understand. Jargon is used by Snowball when he tries to convince the birds that wings are legs In this instance the effect is humorous. When Squealer does the same thing later in the story it becomes sinister. Squealer uses jargon to mislead and intimidate the animals. Imagine you are buying a personal stereo and you don't want to show your ignorance when the salesperson hows you an expensive one with "one-touch dubbing, antistatic mega-bass and built-in tweeters." ✪ How will you respond?

# Do we laugh?

It is funny to think of animals taking over a farm and running it for themselves. The thought of a pig up a ladder with a paintbrush in its trotter is also amusing. There are plenty of comical touches of that kind throughout *Animal Farm*.

We might expect the humour to disappear as the story advances toward its pessimistic conclusion, but it doesn't. For example, Squealer falls drunk off the ladder. Napoleon makes himself ridiculous by switching from Pilkington to Frederick and back again. ✪ Does this make the increasing seriousness of the story more bearable? ✪ Are Napoleon and Squealer more or less threatening because they can behave in this way?

Orwell also uses a form of humour known as **irony** to increase our dislike of the pigs. When we say that someone has made an *ironic* remark, we usually mean sarcastic. The irony Orwell uses is slightly different. It occurs when the reader knows something that the characters do not, and that the writer himself pretends not to know.

Orwell uses irony to show how the animals are duped. It begins so casually that we may not notice it at first. If we do, it makes us smile: *When they came back in the evening it was noticed that the milk had disappeared; ... the behaviour of the cat was somewhat peculiar.* ✪ What has happened to the milk? ✪ What is the simple explanation of the cat's behavior?

After Snowball has been driven from the farm, the irony becomes all too obvious. We already realize that the pigs are taking advantage of the others. As the animals are pushed back to the miserable conditions they suffered under Jones, the irony has a stronger effect. It makes us angry both at the animals' stupidity and the cruelty of the pigs exploiting them:

*The animals worked like slaves. But they were happy in their work ... well aware that everything ... was for the benefit of themselves ... and not for a pack of idle thieving human beings.*

*All the same, there were days when they felt that they would sooner have had less figures and more food.*

*Muriel ... noticed that there was yet another of them [the Commandments] which the animals had remembered wrong.*

*Besides, in those days they had been slaves and now they were free.*

*They found it comforting to be reminded that, after all, they were truly their own masters and that the work they did was for their own benefit.*

By the end of the story this irony has become quite savage. Notice the long paragraph that ends, *No creature called any other creature 'Master.' All animals were equal.* A few sentences later the pigs come out of the farmhouse walking on their hind legs.

# The structure of the novel

The plot of Animal Farm is easy to summarize. Old Major, a prize boar, has a dream about animals rebelling against their human owners, becoming their own masters, and enjoying the fruits of freedom. After Old Major dies three days later, the animals do rebel and drive the humans off the farm.

Life is better until the pigs – the most intelligent animals on the farm – turn Old Major's dream into a nightmare. They devise a political system called Animalism, and gradually their greed causes them to manipulate the less intelligent animals for their benefit.

Led by the winner in the power struggle – a young boar named Napoleon – the pigs set up rules, or Commandments, which they adjust as conditions change. The freedom won by the animals at the Battle of the Cowshed is lost when the pigs become greedy dictators whose brainwashing and mind control lock the lesser animals into worse conditions than before the Rebellion.

Orwell uses no flashbacks or change of setting as his story goes steadily forward in a chronological order.

# The use of repetition

To enhance this simple plot, Orwell uses a pattern of repeating key situations and settings that echo what has happened before, illustrating the terrible changes that take place under the new system. For example, after the animals rebel, they celebrate by rushing to a knoll, where they dance and leap with excitement. This knoll becomes the scene of an execution of eleven animals, where the others are horrified at the "pile of bodies lying before Napoleon's feet."

The patterns of repetition show changes in key characters: when history is rewritten by Squealer and Napoleon, Snowball is first a hero, then portrayed as a villain; and the heroic, hardworking Boxer gets so caught up in the system that he destroys his health.

Propaganda devices are repeated and modified: "Beasts of England" is the first anthem of the animals; later, their patriotic song is "Hymn to Napoleon." The triumphant chant, "Four legs good, two heads bad," later becomes "Four legs good, two legs better" when Napoleon finds it profitable to do business with humans.

One of the most important of the recurring actions involves the plan to build a windmill to supply power for the farm and relieve the animals of heavy labor. The idea came originally from Snowball, but Napoleon later claimed credit for it. It became an instrument used by the leaders to add to the animals' workload and keep them in subjection. The windmill is built, then destroyed by a storm, then rebuilt only to be destroyed by humans. Repeated references to the windmill project give the best evidence of the increasing control by the pigs.

There is a frequently quoted proverb that says, "What goes around comes around." In *Animal Farm* situations come around much like this illustration of a windmill.

ROUND AND ROUND IT GOES

CHAPTER 4
BATTLE OF THE
COWSHED

Chapter 7
The Knoll :-
terror & slaughter

* Chapter 3
Four legs good
two legs bad

chapter 8
Hymn to
Napoleon

CHAPTER 8
BATTLE OF
THE WINDMILL

Chapter 2
The Knoll :-
happy happy!

* Chapter 3
Four legs good
two legs better

Chapter 1
"Beasts of
England"

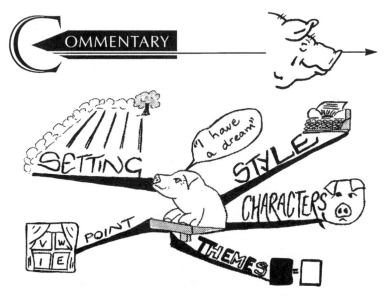

To make reviewing easier, the Commentary divides the novel into chapters, and these chapters into short sections, beginning with a brief preview that will prepare you for the section and help with last-minute reviewing for tests. The Commentary discusses whatever is important in the section, focusing on the areas shown in the Mini Mind Map above.

### ICONS

Wherever there is a focus on a particular theme, the icon for that theme appears in the margin (see p. x for key). Look out, too, for the Style and Language sections. Being able to comment on style and language will help you to get an "A" on your exam.

You will learn more from the Commentary if you use it alongside the novel itself. Read a section from the novel, then the corresponding Commentary section, or the other way around.

### STARRED QUESTIONS

Remember that when a question appears in the Commentary with a star ✪ in front of it, you should stop and think about it for a moment. And **remember to take a break** after completing each exercise!

## Chapter 1

### YEAR 1; EARLY MARCH

◆ Mr. Jones of Manor Farm
◆ Major calls the animals together
◆ Man is our enemy!
◆ Unite to overthrow Man
◆ All animals will be equal
◆ "Beasts of England" – a dream of earth without Man

# "No animal in England is free"

Mr. Jones of Manor Farm does not look after his animals properly. One night he goes to bed drunk. The animals wait for his light to go out and then gather in the big barn because Old Major, Mr. Jones' prize pig, wants to tell them about his strange dream. They respect Old Major so much that they cheerfully give up their sleep to listen to him. The animals are named and described as they enter the barn. All of them come to the meeting except Moses, Mr. Jones' pet raven.

Major does not relate the dream until the very end of his speech. He begins by calling the animals *Comrades* and says that he wants to pass on his wisdom before he dies.

He tells them that they lead short, exhausting lives with barely enough food to keep them alive. They are killed as soon as they stop being useful. Is this because the land is not fertile enough to provide them all with food? No! The land could support many more animals. They live like slaves because human beings steal what the animals produce. If Man was removed, says Major, their problems would end.

He lets this idea sink in while he turns to each group in turn and reminds them of the injustices they suffer. The cows are robbed of the milk that should feed their calves. Clover's foals have been sold outside the farm; she will never see them again. Boxer will be sent to the slaughterhouse as soon as he loses his strength. Within a year the young pigs will be slaughtered.

These opening pages hold vital clues to the way the story will develop. Test your alertness by answering the following questions.

## Test yourself

?      Why didn't Major begin his speech by describing the dream?

?      Notice the way the animals are described when they enter the barn. How do the actions of Boxer, Clover, Mollie, and the cat point forward to the way they behave later?

?      Which of Major's prophecies come true after the Rebellion?

# Work for the rebellion, comrades

Major says that everything could change overnight if the animals did rid themselves of Man. He does not know when or how the Rebellion will happen, only that one day it *will* happen. He urges them to work for the good of animals born after them. They must never forget that all men are enemies and all animals are comrades.

At this moment there is an interruption. Four rats have crept out of their holes to listen to Major's speech. When the dogs catch sight of them they rush to the attack and the rats are almost killed. The animals take a vote. They decide that wild creatures will be welcome as comrades in the struggle against Man.

Why do the dogs try to kill the rats? This sudden piece of action helps to break up a very long speech, but is it there for any other reason? ✪ What might Orwell be trying to point out to us?

After the vote Major repeats that they must fight against Man and everything he does. They must never copy men's behavior, in case they become like them. He gives a list of human habits that animals must avoid. Ideas behind the Seven Commandments are stated.

## Over to you

?      Does Major really think that human habits are evil or is he against them only because they are part of enemy behavior?

?      Major often repeats the same idea in a different way. Why does he do this? Make a list of his main points in    **39** your own words. Reread the speech and pick out the sentences that would look good as poster slogans (only one for each point).

## "Beasts of England"

When he finally describes his dream Major says very little about it except that it reminded him of a song sung by the animals of long ago. It is called "Beasts of England" and is a vision of how good the world could be for animals if they were free of Man. He sings seven verses.

This song has more effect on the animals than anything that has gone before. They become wildly excited. Even the most stupid of them picks up the tune at once and at least a few of the words. ☉ Can you explain why this is so easy for them, when later on they find learning to read so hard?

In their different voices they sing the song five times. The noise is so loud that they wake Mr. Jones. He thinks a fox has broken into the yard and rushes out with his gun to scare it off. The animals run away to their usual sleeping places; the farm becomes quiet.

### More on Major

? Major says a lot about what is wrong with the animals' lives and in what way they need to change. He says hardly anything about how to do this. Why? Is it because he is a "thinker" rather than a "doer"? Could he have said anything to prevent the pigs from taking over?

? Can you see any similarity between Major's way of putting his ideas over to the animals and Squealer's? (You may prefer to leave this question until you have finished reviewing the whole book.)

Everything that happens in *Animal Farm* is "foreshadowed" in this first chapter – except for one vital point. ☉ What is it? If you do not know, the answer is in the next test section.

## Chapter 2

**YEAR 1; EARLY MARCH TO MIDSUMMER'S DAY**

◆ Major dies
◆ Napoleon, Snowball, and Squealer explain Animalism
◆ Hunger makes the animals rebel
◆ They remove the signs of Man
◆ The Seven Commandments of Animal Farm
◆ Napoleon drinks milk – the rest harvest hay

# What is animalism?

Three nights later Old Major dies and the animals begin to work secretly toward the Rebellion. Since the pigs are the cleverest they teach and organize the others. The two boars Snowball and Napoleon and a young porker named Squealer turn Major's advice into a complete set of principles and beliefs. They call it Animalism. At night they hold secret classes in the barn to explain it to their comrades but the animals' enthusiasm has now died away. A lot of them won't make the effort to understand the system and others find it too complicated. Another difficulty is the way that Moses, Mr. Jones' pet raven, keeps talking about Sugarcandy Mountain. All animals go there when they die, says Moses, to a heaven of everlasting clover and linseed cake. The pigs work hard to convince their comrades that there is no such place as Sugarcandy Mountain and that Moses is lying.

The two cart horses, Boxer and Clover, believe everything the pigs say. They attend all the meetings and try to explain Animalism to the others. They are *faithful disciples*.

### Test yourself

**?** Why are the pigs so anxious to convince the animals that Sugarcandy Mountain does not exist?

**?** Think about the importance of Snowball, Napoleon, and Squealer to the whole story. How does their description here fit in with their behavior later?

**?** Can you suggest why Orwell did not describe them in Chapter 1 along with the other characters?

41

# Rebellion!

On Midsummer's Eve the hay is ready for cutting. Mr. Jones goes to the market town on Saturday night and gets drunk. When he returns the next day he lies down to sleep. The animals have not been fed.

By evening they are so hungry that they break into the storage shed and start eating from the bins. Mr. Jones and the four farm workers rush in with whips. They begin to beat the animals savagely. This is more than they can bear. They fight back and chase the terrified humans off the farm. Mrs.. Jones and Moses quickly follow them. ✪ Do you think the animals would have fought back if they had been able to eat as much as they needed before the men started to beat them?

After making sure there are no humans left on the farm, the animals destroy everything used to control them – harness, nose rings, and whips. When Boxer sees Snowball burning the horse ribbons, he throws his straw hat into the fire as well.

 ✪ What does this tell us about Boxer? ✪ Is his hat really a sign of "slavery"?

Napoleon leads the animals back to the storage shed and gives them double rations. Then they sing "Beasts of England" seven times and settle down for the night.

At dawn the next morning they rush to the top of a small hill, which gives them a view of the whole farm. ✪ How do their actions show their excitement? Notice Orwell's simple but appealing description here. They make a tour of inspection around the whole farm but are afraid to enter the farmhouse. Eventually, they do go inside led by Snowball and Napoleon.

The luxury of the place amazes the animals. They tiptoe around the rooms hardly daring to speak. Their awe disappears only when they discover Mollie admiring herself as she tries on one of Mrs. Jones' ribbons. They take some hams outside to bury them. ✪ Why? The only damage done is to a barrel of beer in the kitchen – Boxer kicks it in with his hoof. Everyone agrees that the farmhouse will be kept as it is, but only as a museum.

## What do you know?

?      Why are the animals so fearful about entering the farmhouse even after the humans have run away?

?      Why should they want to keep it as a "museum"? A museum of what?

?      The animals are amazed by the farmhouse's *unbelievable luxury.* Is this true or an exaggeration meant to amuse us?

?      What really triggers off the Rebellion? Do you think it would have happened anyway? Did the pigs' attempts to teach Animalism have any effect?

# The Seven Commandments ✡

Snowball makes an important announcement. This is the day to make a start on the hay harvest, but something else must be done first. The pigs reveal that in the past three months they have learned to read and write. Napoleon leads everyone to the gate of the farm. There Snowball paints out "Manor Farm" and puts a new name in its place – "Animal Farm." At this stage Snowball and Napoleon are working well together.

The pigs have reduced the main ideas of Animalism to seven short rules or Commandments. Like those in the Bible they are mainly of the "Thou shalt not ..." kind. Snowball paints them in huge white letters on the far wall of the barn. They are to be the *unalterable law* of Animal Farm forever.

Snowball has made two mistakes in his writing and spelling, but of course the animals will not notice them because they cannot read. Snowball reads the Commandments aloud and they all nod in approval.

The three cows begin to complain because no one has milked them for 24 hours. The pigs see to this and the result is five buckets of milk. What will happen to them, the animals ask. Napoleon puts himself in front of the buckets. He tells the animals to follow Snowball to the hayfield, he will join them a few minutes later. When they return in the evening, the milk has *disappeared*! Notice the irony here. Orwell assumes the

 **viewpoint** of the animals, although the writing is still in the third person.

**Test your recall**

?     *Do not adopt his vices.* Compare what Major tells the animals not to do with the Seven Commandments. What "bad habits" on Major's list do not appear in the Commandments? Where are they mentioned later?

?     Compare the behavior of Napoleon and Snowball so far. Is there already any sign that Napoleon will become the more powerful of the two?

---

## Chapter 3

*YEAR 1; HARVEST*

◆ First harvest
◆ Work, work, work
◆ Sunday
◆ Snowball's committees
◆ Learning to read
◆ Napoleon takes away the puppies
◆ Where the milk went – and the apples

## *All for one and one for all!*

The animals harvest the hay and corn that will feed them during the winter. Bringing in these crops can only be done in fine, hot weather when physical work is exhausting.

The animals' bodies are not suited to some of the tasks they have taken on. They have to use tools designed for humans and separate corn from its husks *in the ancient style* without a threshing machine. ✪ What other piece of forgotten knowledge returned at the end of Chapter 1? ✪ Do you agree it is *natural* that the pigs *should assume the leadership*?

In spite of their hard work *the animals were happy as they had never conceived it possible to be.* This is because they are working for themselves, not the humans. Each animal contributes what it can to the common effort. The pigs are clever and Boxer is enormously strong; between them they overcome all difficulties. Boxer has his own personal slogan to keep him going: *"I will work harder!"* Nobody steals or grumbles about doing more than the others. There has never been such a big harvest and for the first time it will all be kept for the animals. None of it will go to market. Everyone has more to eat and more time to rest. In fact, this is a picture of how life could be if everyone put the good of all before his or her own selfish interests.

# Nobody shirked?

The animals are too happy to criticize each other. Notice the roundabout way we are told that Mollie is dodging work. She is not as strong as Boxer or Clover, but she could have done a lot more to help. They all want to believe that the cat has *good intentions*. ❂ Why does nobody tell these two shirkers to pull their weight? ❂ Is it to keep everyone in a good humor or is there some other reason?

Benjamin is a puzzle to the other animals. He does what he is asked to do, no more and no less. What does he mean when he says, *"Donkeys live a long time. None of you has ever seen a dead donkey?"* ❂ Is his behavior really any different from that of Mollie and the cat?

**Now over to you**

? In your notebook begin a 'PIG PEDESTAL' to show the changing balance of power between Napoleon and Snowball. The diagram here is only an example. You must

decide the size of the pedestals for yourself. Sometimes
there may be more than one set in a chapter.

**?** What do you think of the pigs so far? Are they already
planning to take over?

 Look over the first two pages of this chapter. What
words make us see and feel the tough physical labor
needed to bring in the harvest?

## Celebrate and educate

The animals do not work on Sundays. They run up a
green and white flag made by Snowball and then gather
in the barn to plan their work for the following week. They
also discuss how to run the farm and vote on the suggestions,
but only the pigs come up with any.

Napoleon and Snowball have begun to disagree; each of them
always argues against anything the other proposes. The pigs
have turned the harness room into an evening study center for
themselves. Snowball tries to form Animal Committees for
self-improvement, but most of them are unsuccessful.

✪ Does this tell us more about Snowball or about the
other animals? ✪ Why does the cat join the Re-education
Committee?

## ABC

*The reading and writing classes, however, were a great
success.* ✪ Do you agree with this? If so, do you agree
entirely or partly?

A lot more space is given to describing the animals' attempts to
read and write than to the rather humorous list of Committees.
Orwell believed that if people are literate, they have a much
greater chance of stopping their leaders from becoming too
powerful. ✪ Why might this be true?

He also seems to be saying that literacy alone is not enough.
Notice how the different animals use their ability to read. The
dogs want to read nothing but the Seven Commandments.
Muriel chooses to read "rubbish." Boxer repeats the same few
letters every day. What does this tell us about their characters?

# "Four legs good, two legs bad"

Because many animals found the ideas of Animalism too difficult to grasp, they were reduced to the Seven Commandments. Even these are too hard for some, so Snowball tries to help them by turning the Commandments into the **slogan** *Four legs good, two legs bad.* (A slogan is a catchy phrase embodying an idea. Slogans are often used in politics.) He tells the birds that their wings are really legs. They do not follow what he says, but they are happy to believe him.

✪ Does Snowball's slogan help the sheep to understand Animalism? How do they use it later in the story? ✪ What does this tell us about trying to make complicated ideas simple?

Jessie and Bluebell give birth to nine puppies. Napoleon takes them away to train them in a loft above the harness room. They will not be seen again until the spring of the next year.

The pigs begin to show their greed quite openly. They take all the cows' milk for their own mash. At least Mr. Jones used to give some of it to the hens. They also seize the windfall apples. The other animals complain that this is not fair. Squealer is sent to persuade them to accept the arrangement.

■ = ☐ He tells them that pigs need milk and apples to stay healthy. Some of them actually dislike such food, but they eat it only for the sake of the other animals. If the pigs do not protect them, Jones will come back. The thought of Jones returning frightens the animals so much that they agree to let the pigs have not only the milk and windfall apples but the main crop as well when it ripens.

Besides being familiar with the events described in *Animal Farm* you need to understand how they relate to the themes that Orwell is exploring. Here are two questions to help you.

### Think about

? Do you think Napoleon might have been stopped if more animals had been able to read when the Commandments were altered?

? Think how the puppies turn out later. What might they have been taught while they were hidden in the loft? **47**

? Orwell called the milk and apples incident the "key passage" of his book. He wrote to a friend, "The turning point of the story was meant to be when the pigs kept the milk and apples for themselves." What do you think is so important about this action?

## Chapter 4

### YEAR 1; LATE SUMMER TO OCTOBER 12

◆ News of the Rebellion spreads
◆ The humans strike back
◆ The Battle of the Cowshed
◆ Animal Heroes

# News spreads fast

Snowball and Napoleon send out flights of pigeons to tell the story of the Rebellion to animals on the neighboring farms. Meanwhile, Mr. Jones spends most of his time sitting in the bar, the Red Lion, complaining that he has been chased off his land. The other farmers are sorry for him, but they do not try to help. They are wondering if they can gain something for themselves from his bad luck. ✪ Can you suggest what this might be? The farmers pretend to make fun of the Rebellion, but underneath they are worried in case it makes their own animals act in the same way. Mr. Pilkington of Foxwood and Mr. Frederick of Pinchfield are Jones' nearest neighbors. They dislike each other so much that they will not discuss how to keep their animals under control. Instead, they tell lies about Animal Farm.

■ = ☐ They say the animals there are *perpetually fighting among themselves* and are *starving to death*. When it becomes obvious that the animals are still alive, the humans claim that they have become cannibals and torture one another with red-hot horseshoes.

The animals on other farms do not believe these stories. They keep hearing rumors about a wonderful place where humans have been driven out and animals manage their own affairs. They too begin to defy their owners with small acts of rebellion.

Throughout the whole countryside everyone knows about "Beasts of England." The animals have learned the tune and words by heart. *Contemptible rubbish* is how the humans label it, but any animal caught singing it is *given a flogging on the spot.* The humans regard it as *a prophesy of their future doom.* ✪ What does this phrase mean?

### Now try this

?       Why would Pilkington and Frederick *not tolerate the name "Animal Farm"?*

?       The *wave of rebelliousness* is really a list of everyday farming disasters. Why should Orwell use these rather than more dramatic incidents?

?       The rumors about Animal Farm *circulate in vague and distorted forms,* yet the song *had spread with astonishing speed.* What is the reason for this difference?

# The Battle of the Cowshed

In early October, Jones tries to recapture the farm. He arrives with his four men and half a dozen others from Foxwood and Pinchfield. They are all armed with sticks except Jones. He has brought his gun.

Snowball has already made his battle plans. First he sends out the birds to peck and drop dung on the men. Then he leads the smaller animals through the farm gate and they rush at the humans as they advance along the cart track. The men beat them off, as Snowball knew they would.

He makes a pretended retreat into the farmyard. When the twelve men pursue the animals they fall into an ambush because the cows, pigs, and horses are lying in wait in the cowshed. Snowball leads the charge, bravely taking on Jones himself. The pellets fired from the farmer's gun draw blood from his back and kill one of the sheep.

Boxer rears up on his hind legs and kicks out with his iron-shod hoofs. His first blow apparently kills a stable boy. This terrifies the men, who run around and around the yard in

**49**

panic as the animals take their revenge. They are bitten and gored and trampled. As soon as they can get away, they run back to the main road.

Boxer is full of pity for the dead stable boy. Snowball sternly tells him that there in no place for pity in war. *"The only good human being is a dead one."* Someone realizes that Mollie is missing, and they go to look for her. She is found in the stable with her head buried in hay. She has been hiding there since Jones fired his gun. When the animals return to the yard the boy has disappeared; he was only stunned!

### Over to you

? Do you agree with Snowball that Boxer's attitude toward the "death" of the stable boy is sentimental?

? Is his concern genuine, or is it partly due to the fact that people may think he did it *"on purpose"*?

## Animal heroes

There is now a noisy celebration. The animals boast about their deeds in the battle and run up the flag. After singing "Beasts of England" they bury the sheep in a solemn funeral that includes a speech by Snowball. They vote to create two types of military medal, one for Snowball and Boxer, and one for the dead sheep.

After a lot of discussion it is decided that their fight with the humans will be named *The Battle of the Cowshed.* Jones has left his gun behind, so they put it beside the flagpole. It will be fired twice a year, on Midsummer Day, which is the anniversary of the great Rebellion, and on October 12, the date of the battle.

### Two questions about "isms"

? Why do people hold yearly ceremonies? Do you think they are a good thing? Can you imagine any circumstances in which they might be used for the wrong purpose?

? Start keeping a list or Mind Map of when "Beasts of England" is sung and the gun fired at the flagpole. Make up your own icons to go with these. Note down whether the animals are happy or sad on these occasions.

## Chapter 5

*YEAR 1; WINTER. YEAR 2; JANUARY AND SPRING*

◆ Mollie returns to the humans
◆ Snowball and Napoleon disagree
◆ Planning the windmill
◆ The dogs chase Snowball off the farm
◆ Napoleon takes over
◆ The windmill will be built after all

# Good-bye, Mollie

During the winter Mollie becomes lazier and lazier. She is always late for work and uses feeble excuses to avoid it whenever she can. Clover suspects she is talking to the humans. When Clover accuses her Mollie, is indignant but cannot look Clover in the face and gallops away. When Clover goes to search Mollie's stall she finds lumps of sugar and some ribbons hidden there. Three days later Mollie disappears. The pigeons catch sight of her between the shafts of a dog cart that is standing outside a pub (bar). She looks well cared for and happy.

✪ Did you expect Mollie to run back to the humans?
✪ What do you put this down to, her laziness or her vanity? Or both? ✪ In what ways would her life with the humans be easier than working at Animal Farm?

# Good-bye, Snowball

The New Year brings such harsh weather that work in the fields is impossible. This leads to more meetings in the big barn. *It had come to be accepted that the pigs should decide all questions of farm policy.* Compare this with the first meetings. ✪ How have things shifted to give more power to the pigs? ✪ Why do the animals accept the situation so easily?

The meetings turn into quarrels between Snowball and Napoleon. They disagree more violently than ever and the animals are beginning to take sides. Snowball makes brilliant speeches, but in between meetings, Napoleon is better at convincing the animals that he is right.

✪ Why is Napoleon so successful with the sheep? ✪ Is it their own idea to interrupt Snowball's speeches? ✪ What is the point of these interruptions?

Snowball has been studying Mr. Jones' farming magazines. He is full of schemes to improve the farm. The most complicated of all is his plan to build a windmill for generating electricity. This will be connected to every part of the farm and run machinery that will do their work for them. The animals are astonished but impressed by Snowball's ideas.

He takes over an incubation shed to draw up the windmill plans, which become more and more elaborate. All the animals visit the shed at least once a day to admire them. Napoleon keeps away. ✪ Why? One day he walks in unexpectedly, looks at the plans, and lifts his leg to urinate on them. He then goes out without a word.

Snowball says that building the windmill will take only a year. Napoleon tells the animals they will starve to death if they do not concentrate on producing more food. They divide into two groups – *Vote for Snowball and the three day week*, and *Vote for Napoleon and the full manger*. Benjamin says that life will still go on badly, whoever wins.

Napoleon and Snowball also quarrel about how to defend the farm if the humans attack again. Napoleon wants the animals to get some firearms. Snowball wants to stir up rebellion on other farms by sending out more pigeons. Then they will not need to defend themselves. The animals cannot decide which of them is right.

At last Snowball finishes his windmill design and puts it to the vote at the next Sunday meeting. Napoleon says the idea is nonsense and no one should vote for it. Snowball replies with a powerful description of what the windmill could do to improve the animals' lives. Everyone is won over, but before they can vote, Napoleon stands up and utters a strange cry. Nine enormous dogs rush in and attack Snowball. He runs for his life, watched by the other animals. The dogs do not manage to catch him, but they chase him off the farm. Snowball is never seen again.

Make sure you have understood the power struggle between the two pigs by answering these questions:

**Test yourself**

? Why does the windmill design become so elaborate? What does this whole incident tell us about Snowball's character?

? *Of all their controversies, none was so bitter as the one that took place over the windmill.* How important was this bitter power struggle?

? At what point in the story do you think Napoleon decides to use violence to win the top position? Could it have been when he took the puppies away to "educate" them?

? What are the personality traits that help Napoleon become "top pig"? What traits ten to prevent Snowball from winning?

# Napoleon triumphant

The terrified animals realize that these dogs are the puppies that Napoleon took away the previous year. They wag their tails to him as their mothers did to Mr. Jones. From now on they will be Napoleon's bodyguards and force the animals to obey him.

Napoleon announces that there will be no more public debates because they are a waste of time. He is going to head a special committee of pigs that will decide everything. The animals will be given their orders for the week each Sunday when they salute the flag and sing "Beasts of England."

Despite their fear the animals make it plain that they object to this new arrangement. *Several of them would have protested if they could have found the right arguments.* Four young porkers 53 do speak out, but they fall silent when the dogs start to growl. The sheep bleat out *"Four legs good, two legs bad!"* and the noise lasts so long that there is no time for discussion.

■ = ☐ Afterwards, Squealer is sent around the farm to "explain" Napoleon's decision. Napoleon only wants to stop them from making mistakes, he says. He will save them from following Snowball's *moonshine of windmills*. Snowball *was no better than a criminal*. Someone points out that Snowball fought bravely at the Battle of the Cowshed. Squealer quickly squashes this idea by linking it with the danger that Farmer Jones may return. Of course none of them want that, so they meekly accept his explanation.

✪ Squealer understands the weaknesses of the animals he is trying to manipulate and brainwash. What are these weaknesses, in your opinion?

At Sunday meetings the platform is now occupied by Napoleon and the pigs with the nine young dogs on guard beside them. The other animals sit on the floor of the barn. At the third meeting Napoleon announces that the windmill will go ahead after all. Squealer tells them that it was Napoleon's idea in the first place, but his plans were stolen by Snowball.

■ = ☐ So why did Napoleon speak out against the windmill, someone asks. Notice that at this point the animals are still allowed to ask the reason for his decisions. *"Tactics"* says Squealer. It was Napoleon's way of getting rid of that dangerous character, Snowball.

### Over to you

? Finish your PIG PEDESTAL. Check that you have included the most important stages in the power struggle between Napoleon and Snowball.

? Discuss the reasons why Napoleon won the struggle between himself and Snowball. Then write them down in order of importance.

? Do you think Snowball ever realized how ambitious Napoleon was?

## Chapter 6

YEAR 2; SPRING, SUMMER, WINTER

◆ A sixty hour week
◆ Difficulties with the windmill
◆ Trading with the humans
◆ Pigs move into the farmhouse
◆ The windmill falls down
◆ Napoleon blames the disasters on Snowball

# Work, work, work

The second year is very hard for the animals. They have to work on Sunday afternoons and put in longer hours during the rest of the week. The crops do not grow as well as in the previous year.

The windmill causes a lot of problems. There is plenty of limestone in the quarry, but the stones are too large. The animals cannot handle picks and crowbars, so they have to find some other method to break them up. After weeks of wasted effort they think of a way. They drag the stones uphill and push them over the edge of the quarry to smash on the ground below.

This is slow and exhausting work. Only Boxer's enormous strength pulls them through. Clover warns him not to overstrain himself, but Boxer takes no notice. He gets up even earlier and returns to the quarry alone whenever he has a spare moment. He keeps himself going with his two slogans, *I will work harder* and *Napoleon is always right*.

The shortage of food is less serious than expected because the animals no longer have to feed five humans. But some of the supplies they need cannot be found on the farm – dog biscuits, iron for horseshoes, paraffin, and so on. How will they obtain them?

# Trading with humans

One Sunday morning Napoleon announces that from now on Animal Farm will sell some of its produce to neighboring farms. This will allow them to buy what they need.

Napoleon's announcement makes the other animals very uneasy. ○ What other recent change did the animals dislike? They remember deciding at the first meeting not to do any of this, or they think they remember. The four young pigs speak out again – timidly this time – and again are silenced by the dogs. Napoleon reassures everyone that no one except himself will come into contact with the humans. He has arranged for Mr. Whymper, a Willingdon solicitor, to call on him every Monday morning.

○ Is Napoleon trying to protect the animals, or has he some other motive for seeing the solicitor on his own?

■ = □ Squealer goes around the farm and says there never was any rule against trading with humans. He tells the animals they are imagining things, probably because of Snowball's lies. When a few still seem unconvinced he asks them, *"Is it written down anywhere?"* They are forced to agree that he is right.

The animals dread Mr. Whymper's visits, but they feel pride when they see Napoleon on four legs giving orders to a two-legged human. In the world outside, other humans still hate Animal Farm as much as ever, but they respect the way the animals are managing their own affairs. They have dropped their support for Jones. There are even rumors that Napoleon will do business with Mr. Pilkington of Foxwood or Mr. Frederick of Pinchfield.

## What do you think?

? Is Napoleon's decision to trade with the humans a good one in the circumstances?

? Why does Squealer lie to the animals instead of pointing out that they have to trade with humans to survive?

?      Can you say exactly why Squealer manages to persuade the animals not to trust their own memories?

# Indoor pigs

The animals are worried when the pigs begin to use the farmhouse as a permanent home. Surely one of the Commandments said this was forbidden. Squealer convinces them they are mistaken. He tells them that the pigs need a quiet place to work in and that it is more dignified for the Leader (Napoleon) to live in a house than in a sty. *Some of the animals were disturbed when they heard that the pigs ... also slept in the beds.* Clover asks Muriel to read aloud the Fourth Commandment. This now runs, *No animal shall sleep in a bed* **with sheets**.

Notice that Muriel isn't aware that the wording has been altered, it is the illiterate Clover who has doubts, and she isn't self-confident enough to insist that she is right. This incident shows how literacy without the ability to look in a critical way at what is read can be positively dangerous.

Squealer argues that any sleeping place counts as a bed. The pigs sleep in blankets, not in sheets, which are a human invention and therefore forbidden. The pigs need the comfort of beds to have enough energy to carry out their duties. Surely none of them wants Jones to return? After this, no more is said about the beds and there is no complaint when the pigs decide to get up one hour later than everyone else.

✪ At what other times has Squealer threatened the animals with Jones' return? ✪ Can you point out the contradictions in his speech to Clover and Muriel?

# The windmill falls

Some of the corn and hay has been sold, so there is not a great deal of food for the winter, but the animals feel that the windmill will make up for everything. After the harvest they work harder than ever to finish building it. Benjamin is the only one to show no enthusiasm.

There are raging gales in November. One morning the animals come out of their stalls to find that the windmill has been blown down. As they gaze at its ruins they are filled with despair. Napoleon inspects the site and then roars out that this is the work of Snowball. He pronounces the death sentence.

When a pig's footprints are discovered nearby, Napoleon declares that these are Snowball's. He encourages his comrades not to let Snowball undo their work. They will begin to rebuild the windmill that very morning.

**Think about**

**?** Napoleon is described as *not much of a talker*. Until his two later outburst, most of his speeches have been plain and short. He usually leaves managing the animals to Squealer. Why do you think his speech and behavior change so much when the windmill blows down?

## Chapter 7

*YEAR 2; WINTER. YEAR 3; JANUARY–FEBRUARY*

◆ A hard winter
◆ The hens' protest is brutally crushed
◆ Snowball is the villain!
◆ Confession and execution
◆ 'Beasts of England' is banned

## A *bitter winter*

The animals struggle to rebuild their windmill through a long harsh winter, knowing that the outside world wants them to fail. The humans spread a rumor that the windmill fell because its walls were too thin. The animals know this is not true but all the same they decide to double its thickness. ✪ Were the rumors really spread *out of spite?*

The animals are cold and hungry, while work on the windmill is now twice as hard. Squealer makes fine speeches to encourage them, but they are more inspired by the example set by Boxer. ✪ Why?

In January the corn ration is reduced. When the potato stores are opened to provide extra food they are found to have gone rotten. During one of Mr. Whymper's weekly visits Napoleon plays a trick to make him think the corn bins are full. Whymper reports this to the outside world. ✪ What *bad results* might follow if the humans knew about the lack of food at Animal Farm?

# The hens go on strike

Napoleon seldom appears in public now and is always accompanied by the dogs. His solution to the food problem is announced by Squealer. The hens must give up their eggs for sale. This causes the first and only revolt against Napoleon's orders. The hens fly up to the rafters to lay their eggs and let them drop to the floor. Napoleon orders the hens' rations to be stopped. After five days of starvation they give in and return to their nesting boxes. The bodies of nine that have died are buried in the orchard.

# Snowball is the villain!

Napoleon wants to sell a pile of wood, but cannot decide between Pilkington and Frederick. Each time he favors one, Snowball is said to be hiding with the other.

It is now discovered that Snowball is making secret night visits to the farm. He is behind everything that goes wrong on the farm. Napoleon decides to make a full investigation. He finds traces of Snowball everywhere. ✪ Do you believe that Snowball is visiting the farm?

■ = ▢ The animals become thoroughly frightened. Squealer calls them together and tells them that Snowball has sold himself to Frederick, who is shortly going to attack the farm with Snowball as his guide. He says that Snowball has been Jones' secret agent from the very beginning. He even tried to betray his comrades at the Battle of the Cowshed.

The animals are *stupefied* at this news. They can remember Snowball's bravery during the battle. Boxer says he does not believe this story. Squealer claims that Snowball's treachery has been revealed by secret documents discovered since he ran away. He gives a revised account of the battle, which turns Napoleon into a hero.

Boxer agrees that Snowball is a traitor now, but not at the Battle of the Cowshed. He does not realize the threat in Squealer's reply. He gives in because *If Comrade Napoleon says it, it must be right.* Squealer leaves with the menacing remark that they must be on their guard – Snowball's agents are present among them.

**Test yourself**

? Who is responsible for spreading the idea that Snowball is visiting the farm by night – Napoleon, Squealer, or the animals themselves? Reread the paragraph, *Suddenly ... Snowball*, before you make up your mind.

? How many methods of confusing the animals have now been used by Snowball? Begin making a list or Mind Map.

? Why do we hear nothing about the animals' feelings about the death of the hens? Is it because they have none? Is it because Orwell wants to increase our horror at the executions?

# The reign of terror begins

Four days later Napoleon orders the animals to assemble in the yard. They cower in terror at the growling of his nine huge dogs, *seeming to know in advance that some terrible thing was about to happen.*

Napoleon utters his high-pitched whimper. The dogs seize the ears of four pigs that have spoken out at previous meetings and drag them in front of Napoleon. Three dogs suddenly attack Boxer. He catches one in midair and pins it to the ground. The others run away while Boxer looks at Napoleon *to know*

*whether he should crush the dog to death or let it go.*
Napoleon tells him to release the dog.

❂ What is Napoleon thinking at this moment that makes him *change countenance?*

The pigs are told to confess their crimes. *Without any further prompting* they admit to helping Snowball destroy the windmill and other imaginary sins. Then the dogs tear their throats out. Napoleon asks whether any other animal wishes to confess. More and more come forward and are executed in the  same way. Soon the air is *heavy with the smell of blood.* (Notice this simple but powerful image.)

The remaining animals creep away to the knoll on which they once congregated in happier times, and huddle together, too upset to speak. Although shocked by the cruel slaughter, they believe the confessions they have heard. None of them questions Napoleon's behavior. Boxer decides *It must be due to some fault in ourselves. The solution ... is to work harder.* He trots off to the quarry.

It is a clear spring evening. The animals gaze at the quiet beauty of the countryside. The peace and plenty implied by phrases such as *young wheat ... thick and green* and *bursting hedges ... gilded by the level rays of the sun* contrasts with the sadness of the occasion. Clover's unspoken thoughts contrast their earlier plans for Animal Farm with the way things have turned out. Still, she will go on obeying Napoleon. She knows they are far better off than in the days of Jones. The most important thing is *to prevent the return of the human beings.* ❂ Do you agree with this?

Clover begins to sing "Beasts of England," slowly and sadly. After the third time through they see Squealer approaching with two of the dogs. The song has been banned, he tells t⁻ ⁻⁻⁻. It is no longer needed because the Rebellion is complet⌐

Minimus, a young pig poet, composes another to be sung instead, but the animals do not think it compares with "Beasts of England."

### Question time

**?** Why does Napoleon make the pigs confess before they are executed? Is it to satisfy his lust for power, to justify the killings, or for the sake of some other effect on the spectators? The pigs know they are going to die, so why should they "confess"? Do they have a faint hope Napoleon will show them mercy, or are they so terrified that they have no will power and will do anything suggested to them?

**?** Why do the other animals come forward of their own accord?

**?** Why is "Beasts of England" banned?

Reread the paragraph *The animals ... to express them.* Why does Orwell place this slow-moving passage so close to his account of the executions? Can you pick out what he does to make the two passages so different?

## Chapter 8

*YEAR 3; SPRING–AUTUMN*

◆ "Our Leader, Comrade Napoleon"
◆ Rebuilding the windmill
◆ Napoleon negotiates with the humans
◆ Frederick blows up the windmill
◆ Celebration!
◆ The pigs find whiskey

## Our leader Comrade Napoleon

 The animals remember that the Sixth Commandment forbade any animal to kill another animal. When Muriel reads it to Clover the words are, *No animal shall kill any other animal without cause*. They do not realize that the Commandment has changed and are satisfied that the executions were necessary.

Sometimes the animals feel that they are worse off than under Jones, but at the Sunday meetings Squealer reads out lists of figures proving that this is impossible.

Napoleon now seldom appears outside the farmhouse. In public he is attended by a cockerel as well as the dogs and referred to as *Our Leader, Comrade Napoleon*. Pompous titles are invented for him; the animals praise him for even the most trivial stroke of good luck. Minimus composes an extravagant poem in his honor, which is painted on the other end of the big barn.

## Napoleon tries to outdo Man

Napoleon is still trying to sell the wood to Frederick and Pilkington. Frederick will not offer a reasonable price so it is announced that it will go to Pilkington of Foxwood. Certain other goods will probably be exchanged with him as well.

Rumors spread about Frederick's plans to attack Animal Farm and his cruelty to his own animals. Napoleon tells the animals that he would never consider selling to a man like Frederick. The pigeons' slogan *Death to Humanity* is altered to *Death to Frederick*.

More of Snowball's wicked schemes come to light; there are more confessions and executions. Squealer manages to convince the animals that Snowball was never decorated for bravery after the Battle of the Cowshed. On the contrary, he was *censured for showing cowardice in the battle*.

In the fall the animals finish building the windmill. Their joy and sense of achievement overcome all the tiredness of the past months. Two days later they are amazed to hear that Napoleon has sold the wood to Frederick. He assures them that the tales about Frederick's cruelty to his animals are untrue. There is to be no attack on Animal Farm. What is more, all this time Snowball has been living at Foxwood with Pilkington.

The pigs are delighted with Napoleon's cunning, which has forced Frederick to raise his offer for the wood. He has also been forced to pay for it in five-pound notes instead of writing a check. When the wood has been removed, the animals are allowed to file past Napoleon to look at the money on the dish beside him.

Three days later Napoleon discovers that the notes are forgeries. Frederick has outwitted him! Napoleon immediately pronounces the death sentence on Frederick and tells the animals to expect an attack on Animal Farm.

**Test yourself**

? Which incidents demonstrate most clearly that Napoleon is getting even tighter control of the animals? Choose two from the following list or find others of your own and explain your choice:
- the animals now agree that executions are necessary;
- the way they accept Squealer's production figures;
- Napoleon's increased privileges;
- the remarks that the animals make about Napoleon.

? Are you amused by Napoleon's going back and forth between Pilkington and Frederick, or is the story now too somber for us to laugh at it?

# The Battle of the Windmill

The next morning Frederick attacks Animal Farm with fifteen men and half a dozen guns. When the humans open fire the animals are forced to retreat to the farm buildings. Frederick and his men overrun the big pasture and the windmill.

While two men work on the windmill with a crowbar and sledgehammer Napoleon reassures the animals that it is cannot be knocked down. Benjamin says the men are trying something else – explosives. After a few minutes the windmill goes up with a deafening roar. There is a huge cloud of black smoke hanging in the air. When it clears, the windmill has disappeared.

The animals are filled with such rage that they charge straight at the humans without waiting for orders. Even the pellets and sticks used against them cannot hold them back. Several are killed and nearly all of them are wounded. Some of the men are badly hurt as well. When Napoleon's dogs attack on the flank, the humans run for their lives.

✪ Why is Napoleon *directing operations from the rear?* Should we take this as a sign of cowardice? He is the only animal to stay upright when the windmill explodes.

# Victory?

The animals limp back to the farm. The sight of their dead comrades fills them with grief. For a few moments they stop at the place where the windmill stood, dejected and silent. Squealer comes frisking towards them. He has *unaccountably been absent during the fighting.*

Squealer is beaming with delight at their victory, but even he cannot distort the truth. Boxer points out that they have only won back what they had before. He has been badly wounded in the fighting. For the first time he is beginning to feel old. There are two days of celebration and ceremony, with solemn funerals for the animals killed in battle. They celebrate with songs, speeches, and firing of the gun. Napoleon awards himself a new kind of medal, the Order of the Green Banner. The animals begin to believe that they have won a great victory.

# Too much whiskey

The pigs discover a case of whiskey in the farmhouse and become roaring drunk. In the morning the farmhouse is unusually quiet. Squealer appears just before nine o'clock and announces a terrible piece of news: Napoleon is dying!

The animals are filled with grief and despair. How will they manage without Napoleon? A rumor goes around that Snowball has poisoned him. Squealer appears two hours later with another announcement. Napoleon has passed a law that any animal drinking alcohol will be put to death.

✪ Who started the rumor – Napoleon or the animals themselves?

By evening Napoleon has recovered from his hangover. The next day he tells Whymper to buy books on brewing and distilling. A week later the animals hear that their retirement paddock is to be plowed up and sown with barley. This is the main ingredient for brewing beer and ale.

About this time the animals are frightened in the middle of the night by a loud crash in the yard. They rush out and find Squealer sprawled beside a broken ladder. There is an overturned paint pot beside him. Nobody understands what has happened except Benjamin. As usual, he will not tell them. A few days later Muriel notices that the Fifth Commandment ends with two words she had forgotten: *No animal shall drink alcohol **to excess***.

### Test yourself

? How many of the Commandments have been broken so far?

? Why is Frederick so anxious to destroy the windmill?

? Does your attitude to Napoleon change when Frederick makes a fool of him over the five-pound notes, and when he suffers from the whiskey hangover?

?  Do these two episodes make his control of the animals seem more or less shocking?
Why did Orwell place them between the executions and the death of Boxer?

## Chapter 9

### YEAR 3; WINTER. YEAR 4; FEBRUARY, APRIL, SUMMER

◆ More ceremony, less food – except for pigs
◆ President Napoleon
◆ Moses the raven returns
◆ Boxer is sent to the slaughterhouse
◆ More whiskey for the pigs

# More processions, less food

Although Boxer's split hoof gives him a lot of pain, he works as hard as ever and never takes a day off. He is looking forward to his retirement in the following year.

Another hard winter means that rations have to be reduced again, except for the dogs and pigs. Squealer continues to produce figures to prove that the animals are far better off than they were with Jones. He tells them they have more food, shorter hours, and better drinking water.

The animals can hardly remember their time with Mr. Jones, so they believe Squealer in spite of the harshness of their lives. *Doubtless it had been worse in the old days ... they had been slaves and now they were free, and that made all the difference.* ❷ Is this true? Are they really free?

Napoleon's sows have produced thirty-one piglets. There are plans to build a special schoolhouse for them in the farmhouse garden. In the meantime, Napoleon teaches them in the kitchen, and they are not allowed to mix with the other young animals. The importance of the pigs is underlined by a new rule: All other animals must step out of their way when they meet them on the path.

By the beginning of the fourth year Animal Farm depends completely on its trade with the outside world. This is the purpose behind all the animals' work, not their own comfort or convenience. Notice the items mentioned. ❷ How many of them are strictly necessary?

Rations are reduced again in February. The animals are no longer allowed to burn lanterns in their stalls. The pigs are putting on weight, even though inside the farmhouse Napoleon has more privileges than the others. Toward the end of the month the smell of cooking barley drifts out of a brewhouse that is no longer used near the kitchen. The animals hope that a warm mash is being prepared for their supper. Of course, they hope in vain.

The next Sunday they are told that the pigs intend to keep the entire barley crop for themselves. News leaks out that the pigs already have a daily ration of beer, and Napoleon receives four times as much as anyone else.

The animals feel that their hardships are *partly offset* by the increased dignity of their weekly routine. There are *more songs, more speeches, more processions.* Once a week there is a *Spontaneous Demonstration*, a parade invented by Napoleon to celebrate the struggles and triumphs of Animal Farm.

**A quick recap**

? When were ceremonies used before to keep the animals cheerful?

? Look at the three stages by which the farm has arrived at full-time trading with the humans. Read the list of things the animals need to buy. Compare it with the earlier stages:
  • Farm produce sold for money to buy materials for the windmill.
  • Eggs sold for grain and meal to see the animals through the winter.
  Is there any major difference between the kind of items bought now and on the two previous occasions?

? Can you suggest why the other pigs should allow Napoleon to have so much more than themselves? Are they afraid of him or convinced by their own propaganda? Is there any other possible reason?

# President Napoleon

In April Animal Farm becomes a Republic. Napoleon is unanimously elected President. On the same day more documents are "discovered." They prove that at the Battle of the Cowshed, Snowball actually fought on the enemy's side!

✪ Why does Napoleon continue putting Snowball down?

# Moses returns

In midsummer Moses the raven suddenly reappears. He is still talking about Sugarcandy Mountain and its everlasting clover fields. Some of the animals begin to believe him. They feel that

since their lives are so difficult it is only right they should go to a better world when they die. The pigs says Moses's stories are lies, but they allow him to stay on the farm without working.
❍ What advantage could the pigs gain by this?

# Goodbye Boxer

There is so much to do on the farm that the animals have to work like slaves. They endure long hours of heavy labor on a poor diet. Boxer never complains, but his shrunken flanks and dull coat show that his strength is failing. He has no voice left. Once again Clover and Benjamin warn him not to work too hard, but he ignores their advice.

One summer evening a rumor goes around that something has happened to Boxer. The animals rush to the knoll. Boxer has fallen between the shafts of the cart while dragging stones to the windmill. Blood is trickling from his mouth. Clover and Benjamin stay beside him while the others run back to the farmyard for help.

Squealer appears fifteen minutes later. Napoleon is arranging to send Boxer to the hospital at Willingdon, he says. There Boxer will be treated by a veterinarian surgeon. The animals are uneasy, but Squealer convinces them that this is the right thing to do.

❍ Why does it take Squealer fifteen minutes to come out to the knoll?

Back in his stall, Boxer is looked after by Benjamin and Clover. He does not regret the accident. He intends to spend his retirement learning the rest of the alphabet.

One midday, while the animals are weeding turnips, they are astonished to see Benjamin gallop toward them. He is braying at the top of his voice. He tells them to come to the farm buildings at once. Boxer is being taken away. The animals race back to find Boxer's stall empty and a closed van drawn by two horses standing in the yard. They crowd around the van to call out, *"Good-bye, Boxer, good-bye!"*

Benjamin cannot bear their stupidity. He prances around them shouting that they are fools. Can't they see what is written on the side of the van? Muriel begins to spell out the words. Benjamin pushes her aside and reads them aloud. The van belongs to a Willingdon horse slaughterer.

The animals cry out in horror. At that moment the driver begins to move out of the yard. With Clover at their head the animals run after the van. Boxer's face appears at the back window. Clover cries out to warn him that he is being taken to his death. Boxer's hoofs begin to drum against the sides of the van. It is no use. He is now too weak to kick his way out.

Boxer's friends call in desperation to the two horses drawing the van. They do not realize what is happening and go even faster. Too late, someone thinks of shutting the gate. Boxer is never seen again.

■ = ☐ Three days after this Squealer tells the animals that Boxer has died in the hospital *in spite of receiving every attention a horse could have.* He wipes away a tear as he repeats Boxer's last words, *"Long live Comrade Napoleon!" Napoleon is always right.'*

Then Squealer reproaches the animals for spreading the foolish and wicked rumor that Boxer was taken to be slaughtered. How could they be so stupid? How could they think Napoleon would do such a thing? The van had been bought from a horse slaughterer by the veterinarian. He had not yet painted out the old name. That was all.

The animals are *enormously relieved* to hear this explanation. When Squealer goes into more details of how well Boxer was taken care of, their last doubts disappear. At the next Sunday meeting Napoleon makes a speech about Boxer. He tells his audience that a wreath will be sent to Boxer's grave, and the pigs intend to hold a memorial banquet in his honor.

On the day of the banquet a grocery truck delivers a large wooden crate to the farmhouse. That night uproarious singing and other loud noises come from the building. Word spreads that the pigs have bought another case of whiskey. They have acquired the money *from somewhere or other.*

**Test yourself**

? How is Benjamin's behavior in this chapter different from the way he usually acts? What is the reason for this?

? Many readers think that the betrayal of Boxer is the worst thing done by the pigs to their "comrades." Do you agree? Think of three other similar things the pigs have done.

## Chapter 10

*THE YEARS GO BY ...*

◆ Years later ...
◆ Hungry, but still proud and hopeful
◆ Pigs walk on two legs
◆ "Some animals are more equal than others"
◆ Pigs and humans feast together
◆ Pigs and humans become the same creature

# Hungry but free and proud

*Years passed ...* The animals are now completely enslaved. Only Clover, Benjamin, Moses, and some of the pigs can remember the days of Jones. The rest are dead. Their replacements learn the history of the Rebellion and the Principles of Animalism from these few survivors.

Think about the attitude and behavior of the animals named. ○ What facts are they likely to hand down to the newcomers? What will they say about Napoleon?

There are many more animals now. Some of them have been bought from other places. Animal Farm itself is larger and better organized. The first windmill is up and running and a second is being built. Business is thriving, but there is no more talk of luxuries for the animals. Hoping for these, Napoleon says, is *contrary to the spirit of Animalism.* ○ What does Napoleon gain from appealing to the animals' patriotic instincts?

■ = □ Only the pigs and dogs have become richer. They increase in number and use more and more of the farm's products, but they do not produce any of the food. Squealer explains that the work done by the pigs and dogs is of the highest importance. They have to supervise and organize the farm!

The animals know that their lives are full of drudgery and hardship. Was it any better in the early days of the Rebellion? They are unsure. Since they cannot remember so far back there is nothing to compare with their present conditions. Squealer's false statistics prove that these are getting better and better.

Benjamin claims to remember everything. Things can never be much better or much worse, he says. Hunger, hardship, and disappointment are *the unalterable law of life*.

✪ What other rules are described as *unalterable* in Chapter 2? Is Orwell repeating the word here deliberately? If you think he is, what do you suppose he is trying to tell us?

Despite all their troubles, the animals never despair. They are proud to be members of the only farm that is owned and worked by animals. When the flag is flying they talk about *the old heroic days*. They still hope that one day the whole of England will become a Republic of Animals. They all know the tune of "Beasts of England," though no one dares to sing it aloud. At least they are working for themselves and all animals are equal.

# Four legs good two legs better

Squealer takes the sheep to a piece of waste ground. They remain there for a whole week while he is *teaching them to sing a new song*. One evening the animals are making their way back to the farm buildings. The sheep have just returned from the waste ground.

The animals hear a terrified neighing in the farmyard from Clover. They rush there and see Squealer walking across the yard on his hind legs. A moment later the other pigs file out of the farmhouse, all of them walking on two legs. Last of all Napoleon appears. He carries a whip in his trotter.

The amazed and frightened animals watch the pigs march around the yard. When the first shock wears off they are almost ready to make a protest. Before they can speak, the sheep burst out into their new slogan.

*"Four legs good, two legs* better*! Four legs good, two legs* better*!"*

By the time they stop bleating, the pigs have gone back into the farmhouse and it is too late to say anything.

Clover leads Benjamin to the end of the big barn where the Commandments are painted on the wall. She thinks the words look different. Benjamin reads them to her. There is nothing written on the wall now except one Commandment. *All animals are equal* **but some animals are more equal than others***.*

The pigs begin to show their domination of the other animals by copying human behavior. They carry whips, order newspapers, and wear the clothes they have found in the farmhouse. All the Commandments have now been broken.

## Now try this

Orwell shows us several times that the animals avoid facing up to their real situation by reassuring themselves that they are "free." Why do you think this them is discussed at this particular point in the story?

? If you haven't done this already, make your own Mind Map of incidents in which the pigs break and alter the Seven Commandments.

# Pigs and humans feast together

One week later a group of neighboring farmers arrive and walk around the farm. They see the animals weeding the turnip field.

That evening the animals hear laughter and singing in the farmhouse. Suddenly curious to learn more about this meeting between pigs and humans, they creep closer. Clover leads them into the farmhouse garden.

They see Napoleon sitting at the head of the table with half a dozen pigs and half a dozen farmers filling the other chairs. Pilkington rises to make a speech.

He says he is glad that the mistrust between them has come to an end. There was a time when the farmers felt nervous about Animal Farm, but the tour of inspection has completely banished their doubts. They have seen for themselves that Animal Farm is run with the most up-to-date methods. The lower animals there do more work and receive less food than any in the county. He and his friends intend to introduce many of these new ideas to their own farms.

Pilkington ends with a joke. Pigs and humans share the same problems: pigs have to cope with the lower animals, and farmers have to cope with the lower classes. He asks everyone to rise and drink a toast to Animal Farm.

✪ What does this say about equality?

Napoleon's reply is equally pleasant. He and his colleagues, he says, wish only to live at peace with their neighbors. The rumors about their revolutionary opinions are quite mistaken. To make sure they believe him, certain changes will be made. The term "Comrade" will no longer be used by the animals. They will stop the Sunday marches, and from now on, their flag will be plain green.

The title "Animal Farm" is to be abolished. They will revert to the *correct and original name* of Manor Farm.

# $P_{ig}$ = man, man = pig

Farmers and pig drink a toast to the renamed Manor Farm. As the animals gaze through the window something strange seems to be happening to the company inside. The faces of both men and pigs are beginning to blur and melt.

The animals creep silently away. Almost at once they are drawn back by an outburst of noisy voices. Napoleon and Mr. Pilkington are cheating at cards. The rest of the pigs and farmers are shouting at each other. Now they all begin to look alike. The animals watching from outside stare *from man to pig, and from pig to man again but already it was impossible to say which was which.*

### Over to you

?     What phrases in the speeches by Napoleon and Pilkington show that both sides now openly admit that the animals are working for the pigs and not for themselves?

?     What is the symbolic meaning of the blurring of the faces of the men and the pigs?

*congratulations! You have reached the end of the detailed Commentary. Spend a few minutes looking at the Mind Map of the whole plot on the next page, then take a good break before going on to look at some review and exam technique hints*

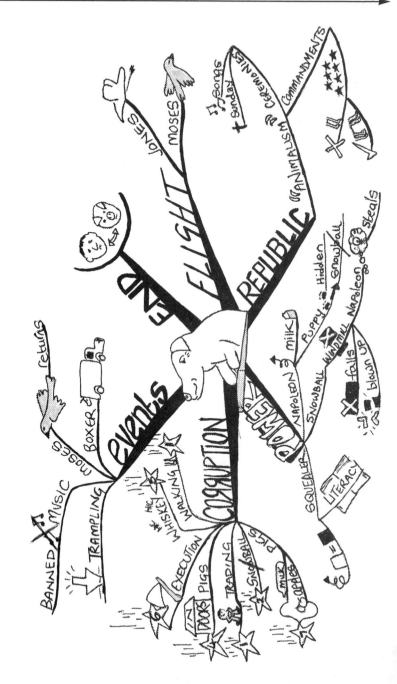

# TOPICS FOR DISCUSSION AND BRAINSTORMING

One of the best ways to review is with one or more friends. Even if you're with someone who hardly knows the text you're studying, you'll find that having to explain things to your friend will help you to organize your own throughts and memorize key points. If you're with someone who has studied the text, you'll find that the things you can't remember are different from the things your friend can't remember, so you'll be able to help each other.

**Discussion** will also help you to develop interesting new ideas that perhaps neither of you would have had alone. Use a **brainstorming** approach to tackle any of the topics listed below. Allow yourself to share whatever ideas come into your head, however meaningless they seem. This will get you thinking creatively.

Whether alone or with a friend, use Mind Mapping (see p. vi) to help you brainstorm and organize your ideas. If you are with a friend, use a large sheet of paper and thick colored pens.

Any of the topics below could appear on an exam, but even if you think you've found one on your actual exam, be sure to answer the precise question given.

## *TOPICS*

1  How does Napoleon use Squealer to control the animals on Animal Farm?
2  Choose two of the characters in *Animal Farm* and show how Orwell uses them to give his opinion about why revolutions fail.
3  What scene or incident in *Animal Farm* turned you most against Napoleon? How did the way Orwell write it add to its effect?
4  How do you think things would have turned out if Snowball had become top pig instead of Napoleon? Would the animals have been any better off?
5  Describe the part played by Benjamin in *Animal Farm*. What do you think of his behavior?

6 Orwell said: *"It is the history of a revolution gone wrong."* Why do you think the animals' rebellion fails in the end?

7 Here are two famous quotations. Choose one and say how you think it applies to *Animal Farm*.

*All power tends to corrupt. Absolute power corrupts absolutely* (Lord Acton, 1834–1902).

*The Nazis came for the Communists and I didn't speak up because I was not a Communist. Then they came for the Jews and I didn't speak up because I was not a Jew. … Then they came for me … By that time there was no one to speak up for anyone* (Martin Niemöller, 1892–1984).

8 What kind of citizen in a totalitarian society does Boxer represent? Give his characteristics.

9 Do the ideas expressed by Moses the raven suggest religious concepts to you? If so, explain.

10 Are you amazed at the gullibilty of the animals? Give examples of the ways they are fooled and misled?

# HOW TO GET AN "A" IN ENGLISH LITERATURE

In all your study, in coursework, and in exams, be aware of the following:

- **Characterization** – the characters and how we know about them (what they say and do, how the author describes them), their relationships, and how they develop.
- **Plot and structure** – what happens and how the plot is organized into parts or episodes.
- **Setting and atmosphere** – the changing scene and how it reflects the story (for example, the animals' enjoyment of *the clear morning light ... the dew ... the sweet summer grass* when they first win their freedom).
- **Style and language** – the author's choice of words, and literary devices such as imagery, and how these reflect the mood.
- **Viewpoint** – how the story is told (for example, through an imaginary narrator, or in the third person but through the eyes of one character – *It was not for this that she and all the other animals had hoped and toiled*).
- **Social and historical context** – influences on the author (see "Background" in this guide).

## Develop your ability to:

- Relate **detail** to **broader content, meaning, and style**.
- Show understanding of the author's **intentions, technique, and meaning** (brief and appropriate comparisons with other works by the same author will earn credit).
- Give **personal response and interpretation**, backed up by **examples** and short **quotations**.
- **Evaluate** the author's achievement (how far does the author succeed and why?)

### PLANNING

A literary essay of about 250 to 400 words on a theme from *Animal Farm* will challenge your skills as an essay writer. It is worth taking some time to plan your essay carefully. An

# THE EXAM ESSAY

excellent way to do this is in the three stages below:

1   Make a **Mind Map** of your ideas on the theme suggested. Brainstorm and write down any ideas that pop into your head.
2   Taking ideas from your Mind Map, **organize** them into an outline choosing a logical sequence of information. Choose significant details and quotations to support your main thesis.
3   Be sure you have both a strong **opening paragraph** stating your main idea and giving the title and author of the literary work you will be discussing, and a **conclusion** that sums up your main points.

## WRITING AND EDITING

Write your essay carefully, allowing at least five minutes at the end to check for errors of fact as well as for correct spelling, grammar, and punctuation.

REMEMBER!

Stick to the thesis you are trying to support and avoid unnecessary plot summary. Always support your ideas with relevant details and quotations from the text.

## MODEL ANSWER AND PLAN

The next (and final) chapter consists of a model essay on a theme from *Animal Farm* followed by a Mind Map and an essay plan used to write it. Use these to get an idea of how an essay about *Animal Farm* might be organized and how to break up your information into a logical sequence of paragraphs.

Before reading the answer, you might like to do a plan of your own, then compare it with the example. The numbered points with comments at the end, show why it's a good answer.

# MODEL ANSWER AND ESSAY PLANS

*EXAM QUESTION*

*One film cartoon version of Animal Farm changed the ending so that the animals rose against the pigs as they rose against Mr. Jones. What do you think George Orwell would have thought of such an ending?*

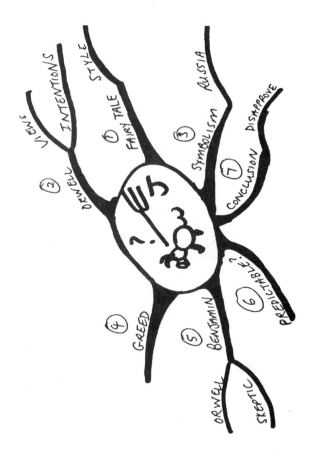

## PLAN

1 Fairy tale - simple style deliberate.
2 Orwell's views and intentions.
3 Symbolism - Russia.
4 Human greed.
5 Benjamin's views closest to Orwell's.
6 End predictable!
7 Conclusion: He would disapprove.

## ESSAY

When George Orwell wrote the book Animal Farm, he did so in a style noted for its direct manner and its easiness to understand. He even called it a fairy tale. He wrote the book in such a simple style so that it could be understood and read by all classes of society, a wide range of age groups, and could also be easily translated.

However, he did not intend this almost childlike style of writing to undermine the very serious message as to the consequences of revolution.

The way in which the ending has been changed in the film version of the book, Orwell would feel, defeats one entire point of his investigation into human society. It also defeats Orwell's search for the truth - the political truth and facts. It also defeats the truth about human greed and lust for power, and the way in which an oppressed people can become too demoralized, frightened, or misinformed to rise up against their oppressors.

To answer this question with total confidence about Orwell's opinion, we must be aware of his personal feelings toward the revolution that took place in Russia and translate it to the rebellion of a group of farm animals. This opinion is hidden in the symbolism of the story and his attitude toward various characters.

Out of all the characters in *Animal Farm*, Benjamin the donkey comes closest to the author's voice. Skeptical of change, quiet and knowledgeable, understanding the changes and their consequences, he seems to hold the same opinions about revolution as Orwell, even though Benjamin fails to speak out until after the death of his friend Boxer.

Therefore, we can ask ourselves, would Benjamin accept the uprising of the animals against the pigs as an expected event! Or would he be entirely taken by surprise if there were a second rebellion!

Benjamin, with his understanding of the events taking place would be able to predict the end of the revolution as it actually happened and no other way. He would have no false hopes about the pigs being overthrown.

Surely, then, we can assume that Orwell was very definite a to the ending of his book and would not have accepted any diversion from the truth.

# GLOSSARY OF LITERARY TERMS

**context**    the social and historical influences on the author.

**dramatic irony**    *see* **irony** (dramatic).

**fable**    a story with a specific moral or message, usually made up by one person (as in *Aesop's Fables*).

**foreshadowing**    an indirect warning of things to come, often through **imagery**.

**image**    a word picture used to make an idea come alive; for example, a **metaphor**, **simile**, or **personification** (see separate entries).

**imagery**    the kind of word picture used to make an idea come alive.

**irony**    (dramatic) where at least one character is unaware of an important fact that the reader knows about, and that is hinted at. Orwell's irony is slightly unusual; as narrator, he pretends to share the animals' ignorance of what is going on. *The importance of keeping the pigs in good health was all too obvious.*

**jargon**    technical language that only those familiar with a subject will understand.

**metaphor**    a description of a thing as if it were something essentially different but also in some way similar.

**personification**    a description of something abstract as if it were a person.

**propaganda**    information given out by a group to persuade people to support its point of view.

**simile**    a comparison of two things that are different in most ways but similar in one important way; for example, "the ship sank like a stone."

**slogan**    a catchy phrase embodying an idea (especially a political one).

**theme**    an idea explored by an author; for example, power.

**setting**    the place in which the action occurs, which usually affects the atmosphere; for example, a grassy meadow.

**structure**    how the plot is organized.

**viewpoint**    how the story is told; for example, reflecting the views of a particular character.

# NDEX